An Appetite For

CHRISTINE SMALLWOOD

An Appetite For *Umbria*

The People, The Places, The Food

Photography by Eddie Jacob

Research and author: Christine Smallwood
Jacket and book design: Grade Design Consultants, London
Maps: Encompass Graphics

Specially commissioned photography: Eddie Jacob

First published in the United Kingdom in 2005 by
Bonny Day Publishing Limited, The Old School,
Exton Street, London SE1 8UE.

© 2005 Christine Smallwood

British Library Cataloguing-in-Publication Data
A catalogue record for this book is available from the
British Library

ISBN 0-9550058-0-9

This book is printed on paper which is acid and chlorine-
free and made from trees from sustainable forests.

Printed by Hilo Colour Printers Ltd, England

Inclusion

No payment has secured an invitation to participate in
this book; a restaurateur could not buy inclusion and the
publisher did not pay anybody to take part. Evaluation
of all restaurants was carried out anonymously and the
bill was paid. In the course of follow-ups (interviews,
photographic shoots etc) some refreshments were
accepted free of charge.

Recipes

The recipes in this book are all representative of the food
served in their respective restaurants. The majority of the
chefs who create these dishes rarely write down recipes and
tend to rely on taste, sight, instinct and experience to guide
them. I have therefore discussed and noted their cooking
methods, had the recipes tested several times, and on the
basis of this research have offered what I feel are workable
approximations of each chef's approach to his or her
chosen dishes.

However, although I have provided basic guidelines,
I have, in the spirit of the chefs themselves, avoided being
unduly prescriptive. Certainly, the simpler recipes should
be treated as free form. As one of the chefs said when I
asked how many tomatoes were needed: "It's up to you.
If you have lots of tomatoes and you're in a tomato mood
then add them all; if the tomatoes aren't good that day
then don't. I can't be the judge of your tomatoes or your
frame of mind."

So don't regard the suggested quantities or
instructions as set in stone. Improvise, use what you
have, play around and, above all, have fun.

Contents

Introduction

Italy has more to offer than most countries: stunning art, rich culture, extraordinary history, beautiful landscapes. However, for many of us, it is the sheer variety and quality of the food on offer, along with the welcome and warmth extended by the Italians themselves, that make us return to Italy again and again.

And it is the food and the people of Italy – and specifically of the beautiful central Italian region, Umbria – that have inspired this book. These pages contain a series of portraits of some of the most interesting characters behind some of the best restaurants in Umbria.

But by 'best' I certainly don't mean 'similar'. Here you will find upmarket restaurants, such as Il Postale in Citta di Castello, Villa Roncalli in Foligno and La Bastiglia in Spello, next to informal wine bars and casual eating places like L'Oste della Mal'Ora in Terni, L'Osteria del Matto in Spoleto and Il Bacco Felice in Foligno. You will find establishments that have been run by the same families for many decades, such as Il Granaro del Monte in Norcia, La Fortezza in Assisi and Ristorante Umbria in Todi, next to newcomers like Vinolento in Castiglione del Lago, Il Cantico in Ferentillo and L'Alchimista in Montefalco. Here too you will find the modern and stylish L'Asino d'Oro in Orvieto next to the more traditional Del Ponte in Scheggino.

This diversity of restaurants is mirrored by the diversity of the people behind them. Many of the chefs and restaurant owners profiled here have settled in Umbria from elsewhere in Italy: Angelo Zarbo at L'Osteria del Gambero in Perugia, for instance, is Sicilian, and Carmine Iaquinangelo of Osteria al Duomo in Todi is Neopolitan. Many of them have had success in other careers: Gabriele di Giandomenico of L'Antica Trattoria dell'Orso in Orvieto, worked in fashion in New York for 15 years, while Renzo Franceschini of Oste della Mal'Ora in Terni is a highly regarded wine dealer.

What all of these restaurants have in common, however, is that they have been influenced by the proprietors' own experiences, and not only their cooking, but their stories and views on food are thought-provoking, entertaining and, perhaps most of all, inspiring.

Many of these establishments are small, and their owners have every intention of keeping them that way, preferring 25 customers to feel delighted about the food and service they have received, rather than 50 merely think the experience was good. In none of them is there a frenzied race for culinary decorations, nor are quality or innovation sacrificed for easy returns: many of these chefs and proprietors are supporters of small, local food suppliers and producers rather than supermarket chains, and all believe that offering good food – and wine – is a duty as much as a delight.

If you have visited Umbria, you will doubtless have been to Assisi, Orvieto, Spoleto and other high-profile hill towns. All are represented here. However, you may have missed such gems as Terni and Foligno. Perhaps our modest efforts to promote their lesser-known but genuine charms will influence your next trip.

Here, then, is a snapshot of the heroes of Italian food in Umbria, some of international renown, others unsung, accompanied by samples of the type of food you can expect to find at their restaurants, trattorie, osterie and enoteche. We hope that this book, and these recipes, will give you an appetite for Umbria and – who knows? – possibly even play a part in helping you plan your next (or first) trip to this wonderful region.

Buon Viaggio! Buon Appetito!

Assisi

Arguably the most famous town in Umbria. Hordes of both pilgrims and secular tourists flock here, so it can become very busy, especially on Sundays. However, culinary experiences are certainly not the reason that most visitors put Assisi on their itinerary; in fact the sheer quantity of passing trade results in more than a few places serving inferior food. There is some good food to be had of course and, as always in these situations, it pays to head for the places that the locals frequent. If you want to escape the tourist masses in the centre of town, head for the Eremo delle Carceri (or at least in that direction) and stop for lunch at La Stalla,

La Fortezza Guglielmo Chiocchetti

La Fortezza
via della Fortezza
Assisi
T: +39 075 812 418
W: www.lafortezzahotel.com

Opening hours: 19.30 – 21.30,
  and (lunch, Sat and Sun only)
  12.30 – 14.30
Closed: Thurs
Holidays: Feb
Covers: 50 (all inside)

Polite, deferential and quietly efficient service. Doilies and spotless table linens. A dramatic vaulted ceiling with paddle fans to cool the interior in the heat of the summer. A menu with a long-standing list of traditional dishes. Diners left to eat at their own pace. And should the chosen pasta dish require cheese, both grated Parmesan and Pecorino will be offered.

La Fortezza is undoubtedly an Italian restaurant of the old school. However, it is also one suited to the mood of the times. Guglielmo Chiocchetti, the chef for every one of La Fortezza restaurant's 45 years, has witnessed many changes and developments in his four decades in business, not all of them positive. To his delight, however, he now sees that, after a period during which people were always rushing their meals, they have *"un po' piu di tempo anche per la tavola".*

More time is indeed being spent at the table, although, equally, La Fortezza has never had problems finding customers. Being in Assisi, it attracts a great deal of tourist traffic during the summer. At other times, however, locals take up the majority of the tables – because they know that Gulglielmo knows what they like. He loves cooking regional dishes – Umbrian-style pigeon and truffles are among his favourites – and Umbrians just can't get enough of them. They come to his restaurant, he feels, because "people at home no longer have the time to make these traditional dishes, so they love to choose and appreciate them when they eat out".

A gentle, smiling, softly spoken man, he loves running his restaurant and the fact that his job allows him to work alongside his family. His wife Tina, two sons Lorenzo and Luca and daughter-in-law Katia are all involved in the running of the restaurant, and the hotel that has been an offshoot of its success.

Opposite: Guglielmo Chiocchetti, chef at La Fortezza since its opening, loves cooking regional dishes.

It's hard to imagine him doing anything else. Certainly, the friends and fans who printed a miniature biography praising his cooking and presented it to him for his 60th birthday may be surprised to hear that any other career had crossed his mind. However, having been born and raised in the Dolomites, Guglielmo's love of the mountains and nature, along with his passion for both skiing and hiking, remain ingrained, so if he hadn't been a chef farming would have been his way of life. "I'd have enjoyed working the earth and raising animals," he says. The fulsome praise you can read in the visitor's book rather indicates that many happy diners are glad he didn't.

In any case, why should he, now that his attitude to eating is once more very much in fashion? *"Adesso di nuovo la gente comincia ad apprezzare la tavola"*, he says. People are beginning to appreciate the table again, to linger awhile – and he is only too delighted to offer them the chance to do just that.

Faraona alla Ghiotta Delicious Guinea Fowl

This dish has been offered by Guglielmo since La Fortezza first opened, and remains a favourite with his customers.

SERVES 4

olive oil as required
1 sprig rosemary
3 sage leaves
1 clove garlic, crushed
salt and pepper
1 guinea fowl (approx 1.5 kg)
  including the liver

2 glasses white wine
1 teaspoon wine vinegar
peel from 1/2 lemon
1 anchovy
4 large slices bread

Mix the olive oil, rosemary, sage, garlic, salt and pepper in a pan. Keeping the liver to one side, add the guinea fowl and cook over a reasonably high heat for 10 minutes. Add the wine, vinegar, lemon peel, anchovy and the chopped liver. Cover and keep on a moderate heat for 20–30 minutes. Remove the bird. Sieve the sauce into a pan and keep warm, or reduce if it is not thick enough. Toast the bread and cut the bird into 4 pieces. Place the meat on the toast, pour over the sauce and serve promptly on hot plates.

Wine suggestion: Red – Rubesco di Torgiano

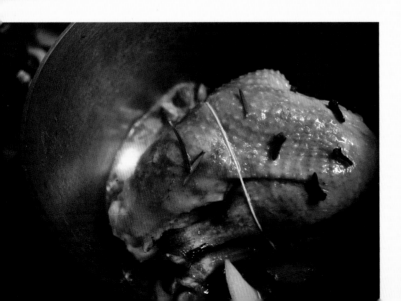

Petto d'Anatra al Ribes Duck Breast with Redcurrants

The sharpness and vibrant colour of the redcurrants in this dish provide a perfect contrast to the richer taste and darker colour of the meat.

SERVES 4

4 large duck breasts
flour
butter
brandy, 4 tablespoons

meat stock
200g redcurrants
salt and pepper
cream

Lightly flour the breasts and brown them in the butter on both sides. Soften with the brandy. Add some stock and the redcurrants, salt and pepper to taste. Cover the pan and leave to cook gently for 10 minutes. Add the cream towards the end so that it is heated through. The sauce should be creamy and thin.

Wine suggestion: Rosé – "Castel Grifone" Lungarotti

La Stalla Benito

La Stalla
via Eremo delle Carceri
Fontemaggio
Assisi
T: +39 075 812 317

Opening hours: 12.30 – 14.30
  and 19.30 – 22.00
Closed: Mon
Holidays: none
Covers: inside 260; outside 900

When Benito, La Stalla's general manager, invites you to compare a copy of his restaurant's first menu more than four decades ago with a recent version, you notice two things. Firstly, that the food has always been simple, basic and good. Secondly, that the only changes between the historical document and the modern menu appear to be the prices and the phone number.

In fact a closer look at Benito's two menus reveals a few additional dishes, but you can still eat here as people did in the 1960s. This is an establishment that is proud of the fact that it's remained pretty much the same for all of its 41 years.

Ironically perhaps, though the menu barely changes, the restaurant does – twice a year. In effect, La Stalla is two different restaurants, depending on the season: inside the cowshed (which is what *La Stalla* means) around a roaring fire in the winter and outside in the garden in the summer.

"The fireplace is a part of Umbrian culture," says Benito. "It's the place where people gathered, especially in winter, and chatted, told stories and generally socialised," – rather as customers of La Stalla continue to do today. In fact, table-sharing around the grill in the winter is encouraged – and popular says Benito. "It's a new way to get to know people."

The fireplace has one drawback, however. Years of cooking over an open fire have taken their toll on the smoke-blackened walls of the interior. Benito's response? Stunningly beautiful red wall hangings hand-made, fittingly enough, in the Franciscan style for which Assisi is famous. Add a few red and white table-cloths and you have a bright, arresting style that perfectly complements the warm, dark interior of the 500-year old building that houses La Stalla. "*La casa e vecchisima* (it's very old)" says Benito, with some understatement.

Opposite: The restaurant moves outside into the garden in the summer where the staff serve simple and reliable food to hundreds of diners.

In summer, by contrast, everybody moves out into the vast garden where there is more of a self-service approach, one that is especially popular with bigger parties. On Sundays at lunchtime you can often see large groups of Italians moving tables around and really entering into the spirit of things.

And you'll probably see quite a few of them. A lot of tourists and visitors patronise La Stalla, but they are well and truly outnumbered by Italians, many of whom come from Perugia. The good-value food and lively atmosphere especially appeal to the large student population from the region's capital – and not just while they are students. "Students from the University get to know us and then return for the next 20, 30 years," says Benito. "They come back to see if we've changed – and they're very happy when they find that we're still the same."

So why is a menu established so many years ago still going strong, with no calls to change from customers? It's simple, says Benito. "What we serve is tasty and healthy. We take things straight from the grill. No unhealthy sauces." And the food really is that uncomplicated: *bruschette*, selections of hams and salamis, beans, straightforward pasta dishes, kebabs, vegetables and cheeses.

But the grilled meat is obviously a focus – and not just because of the appeal of seeing your choice being grilled over an open fire. As very little else is done to it, its

quality has to be good enough to make it delicious on its own, which it invariably is. Benito puts this down not only to the fact that the meat is local but to Assisi's superb grazing pastures. "Good cooking helps," he says, "but quality of grazing is vital."

For all that, grilled meats are not the most requested dishes. They are the *bigoli*, *impastoiata* (see recipes) and *strangozzi* (long Umbrian pasta) while many diners favour the newest addition to the menu, the *torta al testo*, a flatbread widely eaten in more straitened times that is still popular now. Made with only flour and water, it is used as a base for other ingredients, in the same way as pizza. At La Stalla it's filled with ham and cheese or sausages and spinach.

Looking after hundreds of customers is no small undertaking. Benito and his team of 17 are all ready to help out wherever needed, in the restaurant, at the hotel or in the adjoining campsite. In fact Benito himself may serve you when it's busy, evidence, if you needed it, of the warm relationship between La Stalla and its customers, many of whom remark that dining at La Stalla is like being at home. That, for Benito, is proof that he's doing something right.

And of course his customers also trust him not to do anything too drastic with the menu. He won't. "We have no intention of changing anything," he says. "We like being a little island of doing things the old-fashioned way."

Above left: The garden attracts large Italian groups especially on Sunday.

Above right: Benito, La Stalla's general manager charmingly looks after all aspects of the business.

Impastoiata

Benito explains that "at home in the olden days, there wasn't much money for food, so impastoiata was very popular. People would eat a plate of this and it would keep them going for the whole day, even if they were hard at work in the fields."

SERVES 4

1 small onion, chopped	400g cooked borlotti beans
olive oil	1 tomato, chopped
350ml meat or vegetable stock	60g polenta
pinch oregano and marjoram	

Lightly fry the onion. Add the stock and the herbs, followed by the beans, tomato and polenta. Cook for about 40 minutes over a medium heat so that the polenta bubbles, stirring vigorously to prevent it sticking and to break up the beans. Serve piping hot.

Wine suggestion: Delicate Red – Decugnano dei Barbi or Calanco

Bigoli

Benito and his team cook huge quantities of bigoli, one of the most popular dishes on the menu. Their recipe starts with 10kg of spinach. This version, however, is a little smaller, and results in approximately 20 bigoli.

SERVES 4

500g spinach

300g Ricotta

2 eggs

nutmeg to taste

grated Parmesan

Cook the spinach, remove the excess water and chop roughly. Mix together with the ricotta, the beaten eggs and grated nutmeg. Form small sausage shapes and cook them by putting into a pan of boiling water: they fall to the bottom of the pan and are cooked in a few minutes when they rise to the surface. Remove from the pan carefully with a couple of spoons; they are quite fragile. Roll in kitchen towel to remove excess water and reform the sausage shape. Roll in grated Parmesan and serve.

Wine suggestion: White – Trebbiano, Grechetto

Bevagna

The stunning medieval Piazza Silvestri is one of the more obvious attractions in Bevagna, but this small, friendly and engaging town has other charms. Aside from its artistic treasures, it's a delightful and charming place to wander around and, after a quiet stroll there are plenty of refreshment stops to choose from.

Ottavius Edelweiss Biagetti

Ottavius
via Gonfalone 4
Bevagna
T: +39 0742 360 555

Opening hours: 12.30 – 14.30
  and 19.30 – 22.30 every day
Closed: open all week
Holidays: seven days in Jan
Covers: 80

Many of the tables in Ottavius have a spare chair. It's not for unexpected guests but for Edelweiss Biagetti. The chair allows the restaurant owner to sit down whilst chatting with her regulars – or with diners she just wants to welcome. In fact, how she manages to catch up on all the news and serve diners is a bit of a mystery.

But she evidently does both – and with enormous aplomb, as a look through the visitors' book on the bar will reveal. It will also reveal the great – and often alcohol-fuelled – time had by most of the diners before they picked up a pen. "One of the best restaurants in Umbria"; "Great food and great singing!" scrawl people from the UK, US, Australia and much nearer to home. The singing occurs on a Tuesday night when there's live music and party time kicks in, but Ottavius is popular – and stays open – seven days a week. Then again, why close if you're enjoying yourself?

Edelweiss can't imagine an occupation she might enjoy more. It was her husband who started the restaurant but, she says, shortly after it opened "it became a great passion of mine" and she clearly loves every aspect of her work. Her son, Vittorio, and daughter, Lucia, both work alongside her and she's on kissing terms with a high percentage of her regulars.

The Ottavius formula is simple and reassuring: homely décor (there are lots of personal trinkets and photos of the family on holiday); helpful, friendly service; and unsurprising but hearty dishes (sausages, prosciutto, pasta). There's even an apple strudel, made with figs, banana, chocolate and pine nuts, like most strudels but, Edelweiss points out, much firmer than the German version. She also remarks that, along with many other nationalities, a fair number of German and Swiss weekenders like to patronise Ottavius. All of which begs the question, does she have German roots? No, she says. Despite her unusual Christian name, she is 100 per cent Italian – *"Italiana pura, puro sangue"*. She was in fact named after a German girl her father once knew. *"C'e una storia d'amore,"* she says. It seems a touch churlish to ask how her mother felt about this.

The food and the service attract a lively crowd of both locals and visitors, although many of them are also there for Napoleon. Unlike his owner, however, the family dog is happy to sit quietly in one spot, but, like her, he still gets a lot of attention.

Edelweiss has a natural talent for making diners feel at home – but she has worked hard at it. *"Sono qui per loro* (we're here for them)," she says. "We make food they like, we can suggest what dish they might like and we advise them on good wine. If a regular asks for something specific we try to get it for them."

But for everyone, regular or first-timer, it's a question of balance, of attaching equal importance to quality, price, atmosphere and courtesy. Quality at a reasonable price is important, she agrees, because everyone has a budget, but so are good manners. "I always say 'hello', 'goodbye' and 'thank you' to people, whether they have had a Eur12 bottle of wine or a Eur102 bottle," she says. "I'll extend the same courtesy to everyone…although if you buy a Eur102 bottle I'll probably throw in a free coffee."

Below left: Napoleon sits quietly, despite the amount of attention he receives from the regulars.

Below right: Edelweiss Biagetti welcoming diners and making sure that everything is as they wish.

Gnocchi al Sagrantino Gnocchi in a Sagrantino Sauce

An Ottavius speciality, which is on the menu throughout the year and a firm favourite with the regulars. "It doesn't last so we usually make it twice a day,"
Edelweiss explains.

SERVES 5–6

200g smoked pancetta or bacon,
  chopped
sage
1 onion, chopped
olive oil

2 litres Sagrantino
200g Gorgonzola
Parmesan, grated
750g gnocchi

Fry the smoked pancetta with the sage, chopped onion and oil. Add the
Sagrantino. Cook for about an hour, or until the 2 litres has reduced to 2 glasses.
Add the crumbled Gorgonzola to the sauce and stir until melted and creamy.
In the meantime cook the gnocchi. Pour the sauce over the hot gnocchi and serve
with grated Parmesan.

Wine suggestion: Red – Sagrantino (ideally) or a Montefalco Rosso.

Ottavius

This is the most popular main course that Edelweiss serves. It can be prepared in advance and then cooked to order, which makes it useful for both the professional and the domestic cook.

SERVES 4
400g fillet young beef or pork
olive oil
salt
3 slices toasted bread, grated
50g Parmesan

chilli pepper, sliced thinly
bay leaves
onion

Slice the meat thinly and marinade in olive oil and salt for about 2 hours.

Make a gratin with the breadcrumbs, oil, Parmesan, chilli and a pinch of salt. When the meat has marinated, pass the slices through the gratin mixture, then roll up and put on a skewer with a bay leaf and a slice of onion. Grill until cooked through (7–12 minutes depending on the thickness of the meat).

Wine suggestion: Red – Montefalco Rosso

Castiglione del Lago

Jutting out on a promontory and with small sandy beaches, Castiglione del Lago is arguably the loveliest town on the shores of Lago Trasimeno, the fourth largest lake in Italy. Concerts are held in the 16th century castle and there are boat trips out to Isola Maggiore, but the relaxed atmosphere of Castiglione del Lago often inspires much less demanding pursuits. Pine trees grow in abundance in the areas surrounding the lake, and many a therapeutic hour can be spent perfecting the knack of cracking open the small shells that fall out of the open pine cones to reveal the creamy white pine nuts inside.

Vinolento Silvia Fiorentini and Giuliano Zuppel

Vinolento
via Vittorio Emanuele, 113
Castiglione del Lago
T: +39 075 952 5262
W: www.vinolento.it

Opening hours: 12.00 – 14.30
 and 19.00 – 1.00
  (evenings only 5 Nov – 30 Mar)
Closed: Mon
Holidays: two weeks in Nov;
 two weeks after 7 Jan
Covers: 35 inside; 35 on the
 terrace in summer

When she was a teenager, Silvia Fiorentini used to watch Giuliano Zuppel play volleyball on the beach at Castiglione del Lago where they both lived. Now they are a couple and own and run Vinolento, an informal wine bar serving simple but excellent food alongside a fine choice of wine, beer, grappa and other drinks.

Sounds simple, doesn't it? It isn't.

Silvia went to drama school, worked in the theatre, did further study in Perugia, switched jobs a few more times, and eventually became a cosmetics representative. Giuliano represented Italy at junior level in volleyball, had a job in the exhibitions field, relocated to Brussels, travelled throughout Europe, married, divorced and finally came back to the town he had left at the age of 20 to find exhibition-based work in Italy.

And he did. But more than that, he found Silvia – and a new career. She and Giuliano had the idea of creating a point of tasting and sale for oil and wine. It seemed logical. After all, Silvia's family on her mother's side own the highly regarded Mancianti olive oil press and her brother-in-law is a wine producer. Simple, cold dishes such as local meats, salamis and cheeses would accompany these tastings. "Given that I was passionate about wine – and speciality beers from my time in Belgium – the chance to transform this spot together was too good to walk away from," says Giuliano.

The couple took less than three months to convert it, working round the clock. You can see why they didn't waste time: the venue is a real find. Previously a private apartment, it is said that some eminent historical figures such as the brother of the Duc of Tuscany used it in days gone by. A 16th century cabinet was discovered during the renovation works.

Opposite left: The venue is a real find: previously a private apartment, it is said that some eminent historical figures such as the brother of the Duc of Tuscany used it in days gone by.

Opposite right: The choice of wine is enhanced by a selection by the glass which changes on an almost daily basis.

Opposite bottom: The outside eating area on the via Vittorio Emanuele.

Today, with an outside eating area on the via Vittorio Emanuele, a small secluded terrace and a cosy interior, it is both welcoming and relaxed. Customers are encouraged to sit back and enjoy themselves; there are games and packs of cards on the shelves, along with a small collection of books to browse through. The interior walls are used as a kind of exhibition space; the paintings and photos are frequently changed, although the paintings of Giuliano and the one of the couple together, all of which were created by a friend, stay put.

They opened Vinolento, as they put it, "without much experience but with lots of enthusiasm". Still, they learnt quickly. Customers began requesting hot dishes so Silvia got herself a professional cooking qualification and started cooking with fish from the lake.

Silvia is happy in the kitchen, but she certainly doesn't make things easy for herself. There is a constant choice of salads and antipasti, but the pastas and meat dishes vary daily. And she never uses frozen produce. "I need all my imagination on a daily basis," she says, adding in clear reference to her lakeside upbringing: "It's like fishing in culinary tradition and putting your catch on the table."

With Silvia running the kitchen, Giuliano is left to look after the dining room. His English is excellent, a by-product of his past work experience. Add to that his familiarity with northern Europe and you'll find someone well equipped not only to serve Italian customers but to deal with the very different expectations of the many foreign customers in Castiglione del Lago, a town with a massive influx of tourists every summer. Wherever the customers come from and whatever their demands, however, Giuliano is always smiling and unruffled. In any case, he says, "*mi piace il contatto con il pubblico* – I like working with the public."

He has sommelier qualifications from both Italy and France, so don't hesitate to ask him for advice on wine – or indeed beer. There's a selection of beers on draft and by the bottle, as well as a good choice of grappa. A small blackboard on the bar lists wines on offer by the glass and changes most days.

They've also become accustomed to working together, and despite the jokes from each of them about how maddening the other can be, they clearly love it. "*Lo scopo e lo stesso,*" says Giuliano. "The aim is the same for both of us. Our professional and personal lives are very intertwined. There is joy and pain, but the joy far outweighs the pain."

Especially since they have their own territories clearly marked out. The kitchen is Silvia's area, and the dining room is Giuliano's. Well, sort of. "Eating together unites us as friends, so it's an honour to be able to cook for people and to think that you're able to make them happy," says the chef. "When I can, I take my dishes out to the table to see the diners' reactions. Their first sensation when they take a mouthful is important to me. An actress taking her bow!"

Pane Carasau Fantasia Fancy Carasau Bread

Pane Carasau is a Sardinian crusty bread so thin that it is known as carta da musica (sheets of music). It can be bought in good Italian delis, but, should you be unable to find it, Antonio Carluccio recommends a thin, unleavened bread such as Matzo crackers. A good quality Parmesan can also be used instead of the very mature Fossa cheese Silvia favours. Giuliano explains that this recipe, which is a customer favourite in the summer, contains Italian flavours from four different regions of Italy: Sardinia (Carasau bread), Sicily (Pachino tomatoes), Umbria (wild rocket) and Emilia-Romagna (the Fossa cheese). No quantities are given as "it depends on your preference – and appetite".

sheet/s Carasau bread
water
small Pachino cherry tomatoes,
  cut into quarters

wild rocket
very mature Fossa cheese, or a
  strong-flavoured substitute
top-quality extra virgin olive oil

Soak the Carasau bread in water then put on a baking tray in a moderate oven until it becomes crispy. Break it up into medium sized pieces and pile on to a serving platter. Scatter the tomato and torn rocket leaves over the bread. Cover everything with shavings of cheese and drizzle over the best extra virgin olive oil you can find. Serve while the bread is still warm.

Wine suggestion: White – Albello del Lago, Az. Agricola Fanini, or a fruity, dry white such as Torgiano DOC

Spaghetti al Persico e Limone
Spaghetti with Perch and Lemon

This is one of Silvia's favourite dishes to prepare. "I like strong and simple tastes, and with this dish you taste the flavours of the lake. Adding the aromatic lemon rind to the elegance of the perch makes for a simple, but very effective, combination."

SERVES 4

40g butter	olive oil
grated zest, 1 lemon	300g perch
1 glass white wine	salt and pepper
200ml cream	500g spaghetti
pinch Cayenne pepper	grated Parmesan
2 shallots, sliced	juice 1/2 lemon

Melt 30g of butter in a frying pan. Add the grated lemon zest. Pour in half the wine and leave to simmer. Add the cream with a pinch of Cayenne pepper. Leave to reduce.

Separately, fry the shallots in a frying pan with some olive oil. Add the perch and cook for a few minutes so that it flakes apart, then pour in the remaining half glass of wine and soften. Add salt and pepper.

Cook the spaghetti.

Mix the lemon sauce with the perch. Drain the pasta and put in the frying pan, season with the rest of the butter, the Parmesan and the lemon juice. Mix everything together and serve immediately.

Wine suggestion: White – Terre Vineate, Az. Ag. Palazzone Orvieto Classico

Citta di Castello

The most important city in northern Umbria, Citta di Castello is always worth visiting – but do it on foot. There are too many obstacles and hazards to attempt negotiating its streets in even the smallest car. Around Piazza Matteotti there's a good selection of bars and cafes in which to relax and watch the locals interact. There's also a vibrant food market on Thursdays and Saturdays in Piazza Gabriotti. As the birthplace of abstract expressionist painter Alberto Burri, it's fitting that one of Umbria's major art museums can also be found here.

Il Postale Marco and Barbara Bistarelli

Il Postale
viale Raffaele de Cesare 8
Citta di Castello
T: +39 075 852 1356
W: www.ristoranteilpostale.it

Opening hours: 12.45 – 14.30;
  19.45 – 21.30
Closed: Sat lunchtime and all
  day Mon
Holidays: two weeks in Jan;
  one week between Jun and Jul
  (dates vary)
Covers: 50 inside; 35 outside

Citta di Castello is situated some distance from the main tourist route through the Umbrian hill towns. It is however a major foodie destination in the region. This is because of the restaurant Il Postale, which has, in a very short time, managed to acquire most plaudits going.

It's easy to see – and taste – why. This is a well-oiled, smooth-running machine. Everyone, both in the kitchen and in the dining room is focused on making and serving excellent food. The fact that it's all made to look so easy belies the amount of effort and energy required.

Il Postale's chef and co-owner Marco Bistarelli equates the discipline required for working in the kitchen with that of being in the countryside. "You have to know how to behave in the countryside because although it's beautiful there are lots of dangers and it demands a rigorous respect," he says. "It's the same in the kitchen."

Marco's approach is to modernise and update his recipes in keeping with culinary developments and changing preferences. "We have four base menus that change seasonally and then within each season ten out of 20 dishes on the menu will change each month," he points out. But this is not change for change's sake. Marco regularly returns to dishes that he cooked and created in the past to adapt them to his continually developing knowledge and experience. Every day for him is a learning opportunity. Some of his recipes, he says, have taken 24 years to evolve.

This almost spiritual approach to the restaurant's food is balanced by a practical approach to its organisation, largely thanks to Marco's wife Barbara who looks after the dining room with her brother Serafino, a sommelier, and his wife Claudia.

Barbara makes sure that the dining room is elegant and sophisticated, yet welcoming. No detail, however apparently trivial, is overlooked. There is even, by

Opposite: The kitchen at Il Postale is run with discipline and efficiency.

the bar, a small metal box containing toys, colouring books and pencils. "It's important that the children are happy because if they're not the parents can't enjoy their meal," Barbara explains. Also keeping an eye on the practicalities is Serafino's wife Claudia, who helps to ensure the smooth running (and spread the burgeoning reputation) of Il Postale by taking care of the restaurant's foreign PR and helping with the service.

Serafino, meanwhile, is a professional cyclist – or rather, he was. Legend has it that he once shared a very good bottle of wine with Marco and enjoyed it so much that he decided to change professions. His wine list features an extensive choice of Italian wines along with a small, but carefully chosen, foreign selection.

As for Marco Bistarelli, he was born in Citta di Castello and worked in his father's establishment in the centre of town before setting up in this spot a few metres outside the city wall. It's an unusual building. Formerly a garage for postal delivery vans, it was built in the 1920s by a gentleman who had spent some time in Los Angeles. This, Marco and Barbara suggest, explains the name, not to mention a layout of bricks and columns normal in the States at that time, but very strange for Italy. It's odd, but also oddly appealing. The sheltered terrace is especially agreeable; loudspeakers are strategically placed and jazz is a favourite.

Above left: A picture of an old postal delivery van reveals the previous life of the building.

Above right: Claudia helps with service, as well as taking care of the restaurant's foreign PR.

Food, however, is what Il Postale is all about. As with all great restaurants, not only the taste but also the presentation is taken very seriously, or, as Marco puts it: "We don't just prepare dishes, we choreograph the table. *La tavola molto semplice; il piatto e il soggetto*", he adds. "The table needs to be very simple because the dish is the subject. Everything must be beautiful, but when it arrives – bang – the dish must have an effect."

Marco and his team are not about to celebrate, however. This is a serious enterprise and they are constantly searching for perfection. But, Marco insists, they all love it. "We get up early, work for 20 hours in the restaurant, sleep for four hours and start again. Every day. Working in the kitchen is like a drug. I'm surrounded by addicts!"

At the end of the evening, as the coffee machine in the bar churns out espressos into quaint multi-coloured cups and saucers, customers embrace Barbara and enthusiastically thank her for a lovely evening. For a moment, it's no longer about the rigour and discipline of running a top restaurant but the genuine affection that shows how much the restaurant means for both customers and staff. As Marco puts it: "We wanted a restaurant that would attract people from all over the world. We've succeeded."

Above left: Barbara has ensured that the dining room is both elegant and sophisticated.

Above right: The shelving units by the bar contain a selection of books for diners to peruse, along with small toys and distractions for young children.

Pappa al Pomodoro con Gamberi e Triglie Arrostiti
Pappa al Pomodoro with Prawns and Roasted Red Mullet

Marco explains that "this is a Tuscan dish, (Tuscany is only about 5km from Citta di Castello) and I believe that this recipe is an emblem of Tuscan tastes."

SERVES 4

200g dry Tuscan bread
100g celery
100g carrot
100g onion
extra virgin olive oil as needed
4 garlic cloves, finely chopped
1/2 spoon chilli

1kg ripe red tomatoes
50g grated Parmesan
1 sprig basil
8 prawns
2 red mullet
salt and pepper

Soften the dry bread with water, and leave to one side. Finely chop the celery, carrots and onion. Heat the oil with the garlic and chilli so that it is flavoured and fry the chopped vegetables. Cut the tomatoes into small pieces and mix them into the vegetables. Cook gently for about 90 minutes.

Add the torn up bread and cook until creamy, with extra oil if needed. Use a blender to mix in the Parmesan and the torn basil leaves. Adjust the seasoning and leave to rest.

In the meantime, clean the prawns, cut each mullet into 2 fillets and gently cook in a non-stick frying pan with a small amount of oil.

Assemble to serve by putting a generous amount of the tomato mixture in the centre of the plate, topped with a fillet of mullet and 2 prawns per person.

Wine suggestion: White – Orvieto Classico, Campo del Guardiano Azienda Parlazone.

Variazione di Cioccolato Domori: Bianco, Al Latte e Fondente
Variations of Domori Chocolate: White, Milk and Plain

Domori is an Italian brand of fine chocolate and Marco's preferred choice for this recipe.

SERVES 4

4 sheets gelatine
600ml milk
flavours: peel 1 lemon and
  1 orange, 2 vanilla pods
6 egg yolks
160g sugar
30g corn flour

30g "00" flour
300ml double cream
100g Domori plain chocolate 70%
120g Domori milk chocolate
150g Domori white chocolate
selection of butter biscuits

To make the cream, first soak the gelatine leaves in a bowl of cold water for several minutes. Then, heat the milk gently with the flavourings until it is just under boiling point. In a large bowl whip the egg yolks with the sugar and both flours to get a pale, fluffy paste. Carefully pour in the hot milk and blend everything together. Return to the heat in a clean pan and stir continuously over a low heat until the mixture thickens slightly. Remove from the heat and add the drained gelatine leaves, stirring until they are dissolved. Remove the vanilla pod and citrus peel, divide into three and leave to one side.

Plain chocolate mousse: mix 100ml of the double cream with the plain chocolate and melt in a bain-marie. Mix with 1/3 of the prepared cream.

Milk chocolate mousse: mix 100ml of the double cream with the 120g of milk chocolate and melt in a bain-marie. Mix with 1/3 of the prepared cream.

White chocolate mousse: mix 100ml of the double cream with the 150g of white chocolate and melt in a bain-marie. Mix with the final 1/3 of the prepared cream.

Put the mousses in 3 different piping bags fitted with large nozzles. Compose the plate by assembling the different mousses with the butter biscuits.

Wine suggestion: Dessert – Sagrantino Passito.

Ferentillo

The Abbazia San Pietro in Valle is approximately four kilometres outside the village of Ferentillo. Although the church remains open to the public, the abbey has been converted into an upmarket hotel. Try to visit; the views are breathtaking.

Il Cantico Renato Ialenti and Orietta Bellosono

Il Cantico
L'Abbazia San Pietro in Valle
Ferentillo
T: +39 0744 780 005
W: www.sanpietroinvalle.com

Opening hours: 12.30 – 15.00
 and 19.30 – 23.00
Closed: Mon, Oct – Mar only
Holidays: Jan and Feb
Covers: 35 inside; 15 outside

About 20km from Terni lies the beautiful Abbazia San Pietro in Valle. The oldest parts of this abbey date from the eighth century, but there have been many additions and modifications since then. It's now a hotel, and Renato Ialenti's restaurant, Il Cantico, is just outside the gates.

It's an idyllic spot, where much of the surrounding countryside is as it has been for centuries. That was one reason why, in April 2003, Renato and his wife Orietta Bellosono decided to leave the urban surroundings of Terni, where they co-ran the highly respected Il Gatto Mammone, and take over Il Cantico.

It wasn't just the scenery that appealed, however. One of the attractions of countryside life was the proximity to small producers and what Renato describes as his "respect for local ingredients". He is concerned that many small farmers are disappearing because big distributors are squeezing them out of existence. Patronising these small producers is more than a moral and ethical responsibility for Renato though. "It's a responsibility for my customers", he says. This means that he insists on being certain of the quality of all the food that he uses and serves, from the oil and butter to the meat and fish.

To keep in touch with the countryside he changes his menu perhaps seven or eight times a year. However, while he can only obtain, say, wild asparagus for one month, some dishes remain constant, simply because, for example, good lamb is always available from a farmer only a few kilometres away. Which is just as well: it means you'll have a chance to try his signature dish, lamb split into four parts and cooked in four different ways.

Both Renato and Orietta have sommelier training. In fact it was while working as a sommelier in Terni that Renato took an interest in working in the

kitchen. What was a challenge then is now a full-time passion, one that the couple extend beyond excellent cooking to every aspect of its presentation. Each plate is as much an elegant art form as a beautiful meal, Orietta ensuring that the settings are pristine and yet stylish in order to complement and enhance the highly visual nature of Renato's dishes.

Not that Renato has completely abandoned the wine side of things. There is a substantial wine list here run by his wife, but even now, he still likes to seek out quality wines from interesting vineyards around the country.

The couple also like to feel they can pass on some of this devotion to detail and quality to others, which is why they maintain close contact with ICT, a culinary school based in northern Piemonte. The school helps overseas students to learn about Italian cuisine and traditions, although it's hard to say which tradition inspires the current Japanese assistant to burst into his own, somewhat quirky, rendition of My Way at the end of the evening. Still, if it happens while you're there and you've succumbed to the delights of Orietta's extensive wine list, you might even be tempted to join in.

Clockwise from top left:
Renato, the sommelier-trained chef at Il Cantico.

Orietta ensures that the table settings are up to the visual standard of Renato's dishes.

The pasta at Il Cantico is home-made.

Lamb cooked in four different ways: Renato's signature dish.

Farrotto con Fagiolini, Zucchini, Patate e Pesto
Farrotto with Green Beans, Courgettes, Potatoes and Pesto

A delicious vegetarian recipe that does full justice to vegetables at their very best, farrotto is risotto made with farro instead of rice. Renato sometimes makes a tarragon pesto as a change from basil.

SERVES 4

celery, carrots and onion
extra virgin olive oil
salt and pepper
200g farro
100g green beans
100g courgettes
100g potatoes
2 generous tablespoons pesto
Pecorino

Make a vegetable stock with the celery, carrots and onion. Brown the farro and cook in the same way as a risotto with the vegetable stock.

Cut the beans, courgettes and potatoes into small pieces and cook al dente, separately, to maintain their individual tastes.

When the farro is cooked, add in the vegetables and the pesto, and mix until creamy. Garnish with whole leaves of parsley or other fresh herbs. Serve with a generous drizzle of extra virgin olive oil and grated Pecorino.

Wine suggestion: White – Orvieto Classico

Suprema di Piccione con Cilieghe e Sagrantino Passito
Supreme of Pigeon with Cherries and Sagrantino

When Renato's pigeon supplier delivers the birds to him, they're so fresh that they're still warm. The cherries and Sagrantino make this a dramatic-looking dish, especially when served on a white plate.

SERVES 1

1 pigeon
celery
onion
carrot

olive oil
5–6 cherries
1/2 glass Sagrantino Passito
 (or Port, Madeira)

Cut away the breast and legs of the pigeon and make a stock with the remaining carcass, celery, onion and carrot. Fry the legs in olive oil for 10 minutes, adding the breast to the frying pan for the final 5 minutes. Keep the pan to one side. Put both leg and breast into a preheated 180°C oven for 10 minutes. Meanwhile into the used pan, put the cherries, a glass of the stock and the wine. Reduce the sauce to become thick and syrupy.

Slice the meat and pour over the sauce. Serve with polenta.

Wine suggestion: Red – Sagrantino or a full-bodied red

Foligno

Foligno, Umbria's third largest town (after Perugia and Terni), lies between branches of the Via Flaminia and the Topino river and has been a town of trade and industry since Roman times. More unexpectedly perhaps, it is one of the few historic towns not sited on a hilltop.

In 1470, only six years after the first books were printed in Italy, German printers arrived in Foligno with their presses and printed the first Italian book, Dante's *Divina Commedia*. More recently, Foligno was badly bombed in the Second World War, although it remains a

Il Bacco Felice Salvatore Denaro

Il Bacco Felice
via Garibaldi 73
Foligno
T: +39 0742 341 019
  + 39 33566 22659

Opening hours: 12.00 – 16.00
  and 18.00 – 24.00
Closed: Mon
Holidays: Easter and Christmas
Covers: 28
No smoking, or use of
  mobile phones.

"The wine that I like has soul: it doesn't just respect its label but its grape." The translation of enoteca, 'wine bar', clearly doesn't begin to do justice to Salvatore Denaro's extraordinary establishment and its passionate, expansive owner, a wine lover for 43 of his 46 years.

When you ask Salvatore to suggest a wine from his cellar, he knows them all well enough to find a superb one, to suit not just your food but your mood. In fact if you just went for the wine, Il Bacco Felice would never be a wasted visit. But add traditionally cooked food, sourced with a zeal for purity, taste and variety – often grown by Salvatore himself – and you have a culinary treasure that rises way above the bland implications of the term 'wine bar'.

But there's no pretension in Il Bacco Felice. To prove it, there's no menu. However, when he isn't tasting the food and wine, bursting into song at regular intervals, and encouraging an atmosphere so relaxed that guests get up and carve themselves some ham when he is otherwise engaged, or walk around tables looking for leftover wine that is the same as theirs, Salvatore and his staff will be delighted to describe, animatedly, what's on offer today.

The selection of dishes changes every few days, but that's hardly surprising. Salvatore relies on fresh, seasonal produce that spends as little time as possible in the fridge and no time at all in the freezer.

Il Bacco Felice means The Happy Bacchus, an image of wine and laughter Salvatore loves – and encourages. But don't let the almost daily party atmosphere mislead you. The food, like the wine, is sought out with enormous care. It is cultivated, chosen and cooked with an attention to detail that attracts diners and drinkers not just from the region but from as far afield as Germany, Holland,

Opposite above: Salvatore serving up a good time at Il Bacco Felice.

Opposite below: Hard work in the kitchen, tasting wine and preparing fresh, seasonal produce.

Belgium, the US – even Australia and Japan.

The establishment is small with an unprepossessing exterior, but has a steadfast following of regulars and both venue and owner have huge reputations. In fact given its popularity, it is a marvel of compactness, to put it mildly. Getting into the main dining area involves finding your way through an anteroom, rows of bottles, bowls of drying chillies and past the kitchen where the host can often be seen slurping a glass of wine while turning the meat on the grill or chopping up vegetables. The kitchen itself is tiny (if a couple of guests wander in it's full) and yet, somehow, quite extraordinary food comes out of it.

Once they do find a table, how the guests all fit into Salvatore's wine bar is something of a mystery, let alone how they find the room to add their comments to the many scribbled on the walls. Salvatore positively approves of this epidemic of graffiti, which is hardly surprising: it's his enthusiasm for seeking out authenticity and flavour that inspires the uniformly approving messages. As he says; "What's important in a recipe is the standard of the basic ingredients. Tomatoes, aubergines and garlic are all life choices." He adds,; "Today I was sent salt from Sicily and garlic – a particular garlic from Nubia, a small village next to Trapani. It smells amazing." Similarly the cheese served could be any of a number cultivated in a time-honoured fashion for hundreds of years: a Pecorino, say, from Sicily, Tuscany or Sardinia.

He never buys from supermarkets, but from trusted small producers.

Above: Salvatore cultivates a huge variety of produce in his large garden, predominantly for his enoteca.

However, quality control is even easier if you can grow your own produce. And he does that too. It's all cultivated predominantly for the enoteca and arrives with Salvatore at the restaurant as the day begins. Luckily he has a big garden. "I grow pumpkins, courgettes, artichokes, cardoons, wild chicory and a number of traditional wild Umbrian herbs," he says, adding that he loves cooking with his own home-grown chillies. This is no casual boast: he grows (at the last count) 55 different types of chilli, not to mention 54 types of tomato and black and white mulberries that he uses to make jams for tarts. He also raises chickens – chickens that he agrees are smaller, lighter and take a lot longer to mature than their industrially produced counterparts but which are consequently delicious. If they're on the menu, try them, he says, cooked with chillies and truffles. If not, make sure you're there when they are. It's worth the wait.

And then there are the pigs. Visitors to Salvatore's home near Bevagna who find their way past the Charles Heidseck champagne buckets, piles of boxes, feed bags, Tommy the cat, Rosa the dog and, bizarrely, a US mail box, cannot fail to notice the pigs. They're fed a mixture of grains and chickpeas, showered twice a day with a hosepipe and given their very own cherry tree from which they love to pick morsels, standing up on their hind legs.

And of course, they taste wonderful – or they did until he grew so fond of them that he no longer had the heart to slaughter them. He now keeps them as pets. Nevertheless, using his own or equally fine porcine examples, he has gained a reputation for production of quite superior pork dishes – one of which may have inspired the customer who called him "the king of pork and the king of cork".

Salami especially is a subject dear to his heart. "It's very hard to make good salami," he explains. "The colour is often good, but that doesn't guarantee flavour. In fact I don't believe you can find good salami in shops any more. The salami I make with a friend uses the whole pig and it's made without preservatives. It has the taste and that is what matters."

His knowledge of local foods is astonishing – all the more so when you realise that Umbria is not his place of birth – or even upbringing. In fact, he first stopped there on his way from home in Sicily to study economics.

He may not come from Umbria but he does know a cooking culture when he sees one. "The cooking that you find in Umbria is long-established but also creative, innovative cooking that represents colour, sensations – all the necessary techniques of cooking – yet still maintains its soul," he says. "Cooking is still centred around the olive here; and the olive and its oil are very important to me. Also, the wild seasonal vegetables are astoundingly good."

Had the Slow Food movement not existed, you feel that Salvatore Denaro's evangelical championing of small specialist producers might, on its own have spread the word. As it is, he is a member of, and actively proselytises for, a movement that has helped to ensure the survival of producers of once endangered joys such as Trasimeno beans, Tuscan salami or *capocollo* made in Puglia with almond shells. And the message is getting across. Small producers are finding a market through Salvatore and like-minded restaurant and bar owners. And he sees hope for the quality that is his obsession. "Agriculture has become industrial. Our entire food system has changed to one in which there are no longer any smells, colours or flavours," he says. "In big towns there are still small specialist shops but everything else keeps getting bigger and less interesting: 'standard' in fact. But I think we have begun to realise that the true riches are in the earth."

And with produce this good you don't need to over-elaborate. Highlights from the kitchen, and his marvellous cooks Giulita and Tiziana, include a dish of pork cooked with olive oil and white wine, served with boiled, sliced and oiled potatoes and green beans. Or a handful of Salvatore's home-grown vegetables and herbs, boiled and sautéed in a pan with chillies in oil and added to grilled or oven-cooked lamb. Or quite sensational stuffed courgettes. Or a simple but mouth-watering chicken and potato tart.

Salvatore is passionate about his wine bar. His commitment is such that for the first seven of its 12 years he ran it by himself – working until two in the morning and sleeping above it. Even now he often puts in more hours than many of us would spend awake. Why does he work so hard? "This is the life I've chosen. I sometimes dream of taking a year off but the wine bar comes first because this is what I love: food and wine – and educating people, conveying an understanding of what excellence means." This he takes quite literally, regularly chatting to guests about the food and wine they've ordered, even tasting it with them or bringing over a bottle he's opened for someone else but he feels they have to try.

But, for Salvatore, memory is even more important than education – a memory of smells and tastes. And that brings us back to his love of wine. "When I taste a wine I want to be able to describe it, to give people information that they can understand and use. So in red wine we find red fruits: fruits of the forest, strawberries, raspberries, blueberries, blackberries. But in white wine we find white perfumes, so we'll find pulp of peaches, almonds, apples, bananas, mango, papaya, depending on the concentration of the wine. If you recognise that description in a wine you have tried, you have an association; you remember it. After all, if you don't remember, how can you describe it?"

So how would he describe Il Bacco Felice? "A place where the wine has the right to be next to the food – food and cooking that are traditional. Food and cooking of quality".

Food and cooking that, like his wine, have soul.

Opposite above: The kitchen is tiny, yet somehow quite extraordinary food comes out of it.

Opposite below: There is an epidemic of graffiti; diners are encouraged to add their comments to the walls – if they can find any space.

Panzanella Bread Salad

*This is dramatically served from a gargantuan platter by Salvatore, garnished with
enormous basil leaves, and often accompanied by a top quality buffalo mozzarella
and desalinated anchovies.*

SERVES 4

6 wholemeal barley rolls, or the
  equivalent amount of wholemeal
  bread, on the stale side
500g cherry tomatoes
celery heart (the sweetest part)
20g olives, stones removed
1 small onion or large handful
  of chives

dried oregano
fresh mint
fresh basil
20g extra virgin olive oil per person
vinegar
white pepper
salt

Break up the bread into smallish pieces and put into the bottom of the serving
bowl. Mix up enough cold water with 15–20% vinegar to dampen the bread,
and pour over. Squeeze out and discard any excess liquid; the bread should
simply be softened, not soaked. Add salt and white pepper. Halve the cherry
tomatoes, salt them and add to the bread. Slice the celery heart quite thickly and
add to the bowl. Cover with the oil, the torn basil, the olives, oregano, the finely
chopped onion, or chives and abundant extra virgin olive oil.

    Keep in a cool place or in the fridge and garnish with whole basil leaves
before serving.

Wine suggestion: White – Orvieto Classico or Grechetto di Colli Martani

Parmigiana di Melanzane

An aubergine parmigiana – layers of aubergine with tomato sauce and cheese – is usually assembled in a baking dish and finished by baking in the oven. Salvatore's version uses tomato slices and is simply heated through in a frying pan to be served lukewarm rather than piping hot, which makes it an ideal adaptation for warmer weather.

SERVES 6

breadcrumbs
2 large aubergines, sliced
  approximately 1cm thick
300g tomatoes, sliced quite finely
oil

seasoning
50g Parmesan
basil, to taste
3 hard boiled eggs, chopped

Generously salt the aubergine slices and leave for about 30 minutes so that the bitter juices are extracted. Wipe the slices dry of both water and salt. Gently fry the slices in vegetable oil (not olive oil) and dry them on kitchen towels after frying to remove excess grease.

Put the breadcrumbs on the bottom of the pan, without adding any oil. Cover the crumbs with one layer of aubergine slices, and then the tomato slices. Sprinkle over the chopped basil and then grate over the Parmesan. Cover with the chopped eggs, and finally layer over the remaining aubergine slices. Cook gently to heat through and ensure that the breadcrumbs at the bottom are crispy. This should take a matter of minutes.

Put a serving dish over the frying pan and reverse the contents onto it. This can be refrigerated for 1–2 hours but is best eaten neither too hot nor too cold.

Wine suggestion: Medium–bodied Red – Rosso di Franciacorta, Rosso dell'Etna or Montefalco Rosso

Villa Roncalli Marialuisa Scolastra

Villa Roncalli
viale Roma 25
Foligno
T: +39 0742 391 091

Opening hours: 20.00 – 22.30
  and 13.00 – 15.00 (Sun only)
Closed: Mon
Holidays: from 7/8 Jan for
  about ten days and from
  8–end Aug. Hotel always open
Covers: 50. Ten rooms

Slow food. In every sense of the term. The first time I ate at Villa Roncalli, I didn't receive my first course until well over an hour after ordering – but it wasn't because of inefficiency. As it was the first time I'd eaten there the chef was anxious for me to get a feel for her type of cooking, so she insisted I try a few taster plates – with accompanying glasses of wine, of course. "Sometimes on the menu there's something that grabs you and other times it doesn't inspire to that level," she explains. "I want people to know what sort of dishes to expect."

You should definitely eat here – if you have time. Time to sit back, relax and enjoy every mouthful. The food is superb. However, it's served at a careful, deliberate pace that matches the tranquil, sedate, somewhat other-worldly setting – because everyone is an honoured guest of Villa Roncalli's fine chef.

The ultra-attentive host in question is Marialuisa Scolastra whose family have run Villa Roncalli for 20 years. Her late mother was chef before her, and her father still diligently tends the garden and makes all the pork products. She may have the calm demeanour of a Vermeer portrait but it belies an intense, passionate woman. And a perfectionist.

For this is not a job that Marialuisa has taken on half-heartedly. She lives and breathes every aspect of Villa Roncalli. Sometimes she can barely sleep for going over the day's cooking in her head, reliving what she created that day and with what ingredients.

She agrees she has to relax because "if I don't spend time away from the kitchen I can't be creative when I'm there". But it's a somewhat unconventional form of escape. *"Ho una grande passione per i libri antichi, per le vecchie ricette,"* she says. "I read an awful lot and I love old recipe books. When I retire each day for

Opposite above: The terrace at Villa Roncalli where diners enjoy superb food served at a careful, deliberate pace.

Opposite below: The aroma of freshly baked bread is one of the many wonderful smells pervading the Villa.

a couple of hours, I think about the produce I've bought that morning and how I can transform it. I think about my mother and all the things we did together and inspiration comes to me."

If it wasn't for the heart and passion that goes into her cooking, her approach could almost be described as cerebral gastronomy. She certainly feels strongly about the importance of technique and training in the kitchen. "Knowledge is fundamentally important; I like to know everything," she says.

She is, she adds, lucky that there's such excellent produce in Umbria, although she worries that it's becoming harder and harder for small producers to stay solvent. Nevertheless, in a world where so many people opt for farmed fish, she has wild fish delivered to Villa Roncalli every day – fresh, tasty, healthy food that she enjoys cooking simply with beans and vegetables.

She also loves making pasta, but naturally she has to do it the hard way. *"Io faccio una pasta ancora con il matterello e con molte uove,"* she admits. "I still make it with a rolling pin and lots of eggs. It takes a lot of effort and it's tiring but I just love the smell of the dough, of the eggs and flour."

Those aren't the only wonderful smells. Should you stay overnight at the villa, baking aromas of bread, croissants and perhaps cakes will fire up your appetite for breakfast, no matter how much you may have eaten the night before. The jam is a real fruit punch to the taste buds too: Marialuisa spreads out a rich fruit compote on large baking dishes, and sprinkles over broken cinnamon sticks and sugar. Then she pours on some freshly squeezed lemon and orange juice with a generous splash of rum and Sambuca. This is all put into a very low oven for as long as six hours to intensify the taste. The alcohol burns off – but it still leaves a bit of a kick to accompany that morning cappuccino.

You can tell that taste, smell, colour and technique are the building blocks of Marialuisa's cooking – but there is something else. She feels that women have a very different approach from that of men. "We're better with subtle, delicate flavours," she says, adding, not entirely as a joke: "We don't feel the need to throw chilli into everything."

In the garden too she feels that when women nurture seedlings they're less likely to be picked before they're ready. And she should know: she dedicates a considerable amount of time and energy to her garden and picks produce most days for immediate inclusion in her dishes.

Not surprisingly most of her employees are women, foremost among them Agnes, who is Swiss, and who takes care of the admin and generally keeps the place on track in a multilingual, efficient and charming way. But that doesn't mean that Marialuisa sticks to the kitchen and garden. Somehow she finds time to attend to every detail, not just in the dining room but also in the ten bedrooms

Clockwise from top left: Marialuisa dedicates considerable time to the cultivation of produce in the Villa's garden.

There is a tranquil, sedate and somewhat other-worldly feel to Villa Roncalli.

Produce is picked most days for immediate inclusion in the dishes offered.

Marialuisa finds time to deal with every aspect of Villa Roncalli, not just the kitehcn and garden.

that are the hotel side of Villa Roncalli. She arranges the beautiful and sizable vases of flowers, ensures that the candles are the right colour and is also very particular about which plates are used for each dish. She even takes responsibility for the wine list because, as she says, "I love wine. *Amo molto il vino, tantissimo.*"

In the winter, most diners are from the surrounding area – Foligno, Spello, Perugia – and at other times from elsewhere in Italy. Only a few foreigners find their way here. In any case, Marialuisa doesn't try to have a full dining room every night. She likes to be able to keep up with every table and that becomes difficult with too many people. She likes to pop out of the kitchen occasionally to see if her diners are happy, although quite often she doesn't need to: they pop into the kitchen to thank her.

It's not surprising. Marialuisa brings huge quantities of care and talent to everything that she touches and unfailingly serves up first-class food full of flavour and artistry. It's something she was born into, after all. "I remember rolling out pasta with my mother when I was very young. It's not possible to suddenly become a chef at the age of 40 having been, say, a teacher up until then. It's cultural."

So, yes, it's slow food all right, but it's more than worth the wait. Marialuisa

Above: Marialuisa puts her heart and soul into her cooking but feels strongly about the importance of technique and training in the kitchen.

takes her food seriously and the result is a remarkably good restaurant. She admits that, if it weren't economic madness, she would happily forego a charge just to be sure her customers left with a good memory of her. "The cooking is a bit like my mirror image," she explains. "It's what I feel, and I think that people who eat here feel a bit of me. *Il momento della tavola e uno dei momenti piu belli*. Times spent at the table are the most beautiful moments. My mother and father taught me that."

Above: Fresh produce is delivered to the Villa every day.

Passatina di Patate
Creamy Potatoes with Clams and Sea Bream

Marialuisa loves cooking with fish and a delivery of wild (never farmed) fish is made to Villa Roncalli most days. This is a simple dish that's easy to prepare at home.

SERVES 4

3 big potatoes
70g butter
400ml milk, warmed
50g Parmesan
nutmeg
salt and pepper as needed
olive oil

250g clams
1 sea bream
1 clove of garlic
chopped parsley
sprig of rosemary
1 slice of bread

Boil the potatoes, peel them and mash thoroughly with the butter. Add the warm milk, mix together with a whisk and cook over a gentle heat for about 10 minutes so that the texture of the mash becomes even. Season with the Parmesan, grated nutmeg, salt, pepper and olive oil to taste.

In the meantime cook the clams in a pan. Flash-fry the sea bream with oil, garlic, parsley and rosemary. Shell the clams. Lightly toast the bread.

Put the passatina of potatoes in the centre of a plate together with the shelled clams, the sea bream and the toasted bread.

Garnish with the parsley.

Wine suggestion: White – Gregante di Caprai

Torta al Caffe Coffee Cake

"My coffee cake is exquisite. The recipe has been in my family for generations and many, many people have asked me for it, but I've never disclosed it before."

SERVES 4

100g butter
150g caster sugar
4 eggs
5g vanilla seeds
pinch salt

2 cups cool espresso coffee
300g flour
1 glass full fat milk
1 spoon rum
20g baking powder

Soften the butter at room temperature and cream with the sugar until light and fluffy. Mix in the beaten eggs, vanilla, salt, coffee, flour, milk, rum and finally the baking powder. This should result in a creamy mixture.

Cook in the oven at 170°C in dariol moulds or muffin cases. Do not overfill the moulds as these rise quite significantly. Check with a fine skewer after about 25 minutes to see if done.

Serve 2 cakes per person with caramel sauce and cream or custard if desired.

Caramel sauce: 1 glass water and 300g sugar – bring to the boil until it becomes golden, add a glass of fresh cream. Bring back to the boil for a few minutes.

Chantilly cream or confectioner's custard (flavoured with some rum):
put around the caramel sauce and sprinkle over some bitter cocoa powder.

Wine suggestion: Dessert – Vin Santo or Moscato di Pantelleria

Gubbio

Medieval Gubbio was a well-known ceramics centre and home of one of the greatest ceramicists, Mastro Giorgio Andreoli. This tradition lives on through the numerous ceramics shops in town displaying huge arrays of pots, platters and assorted pottery. There is a large and lively market on Tuesday.

La Fornace di Mastro Giorgio Giuseppe Rosati
La Madia di Giuseppe Giuseppe Rosati

La Fornace di Mastro Giorgio
via Mastro Giorgio 2
Gubbio
T: +39 075 922 1836
W: www.rosatihotels.com

Opening hours: 12.00 – 14.30
 and 19.30 – 22.30
Closed: Tues, and lunchtime Wed
Holidays: 10–31 Jan;
 one week in Jul (dates vary)
Covers: 140

La Madia di Giuseppe
via Mastro Giorgio 2
Gubbio

Opening hours: 10.30 – 20.00
 (Wed, Thurs and Sun);
 10.30 – 23.30 (Fri and Sat)
Closed: Mon and Tues
Holidays: 10–31 Jan; one week
 in Jul (dates vary)
Covers: 40
No smoking

La Fornace di Mastro Giorgio first opened in 1982. Its walls, however, have been in place since the 14th century. At that time they were part of the ceramics factory owned by one of Gubbio's most famous names, the great ceramic artist Giorgio Andreoli. Hence the *fornace*, or furnace, of Master Giorgio.

However, when Giuseppe Rosati took over in 1997 the restaurant had long since closed. He was, in effect, starting from scratch. He had a few advantages, however. He had spent time in London, and counts culinary masters such as Michel Roux, Marco Pierre White and Giorgio Locatelli as friends. He also comes from a family of restaurateurs and knows how important it is to understand his clients. Just watch him. He visits every occupied table at least once and tries to spend quality time with his regulars.

But he also knows that people don't enjoy their evening just because they've had a chat with the owner. This is why he was delighted when his friend and colleague, the effervescent Mirko Crocioni, agreed to move from Citta di Castello to head up the kitchen. You can't miss Mirko. One of his mild eccentricities is to change his glasses to mark the season. He wears red glasses in the summer (as they enhance his tan) but black and white ones from September to May.

Mirko's strength as a chef, says Giuseppe, is his understanding of the composition of a dish: the way all the ingredients – herbs, spices, meat, vegetables – come together to make a harmonious whole. And Mirko proves it time and again as a large part of the menu changes seasonally and new dishes are developed. Mirko comes up with the recipes, Giuseppe assesses them, appropriate wines are discussed. Daily specials are offered on Fridays, Saturdays and Sundays. Mirko somehow also has time to make fresh pasta every day, along with two or three different types of bread.

La Fornace di Mastro Giorgio has a strong local following, to which the adjoining wine bar, La Madia di Giuseppe, contributes. Although it was set up to focus on wine (Giuseppe is a sommelier) it also acts as an entry point for the restaurant. The idea is that first-timers – especially younger customers – will enjoy the cheeses, salamis and salads in the enoteca and consider moving up to the wider range offered by the restaurant – if, that is, they're not still marvelling at the choice of wines by the glass offered in the enoteca, a selection which changes every week.

Luckily, the restaurant also benefits from Giuseppe's wine expertise. In fact he has tried to simplify his wine list in the restaurant, reducing it from 500 to 200-odd choices: 150 important labels and 50 that are "more commercial: good but not too expensive", as he puts it. The wines on offer are predominantly Italian, a reflection of Giuseppe's delight in visiting vineyards and wine producers. "When you speak directly with them you feel their passion for their wine, their work, their land and grapes, and this passion is so important," he says.

So which is it to be? Wine bar or restaurant? In fact, there is a third dining option at Giuseppe Rosati's establishment. Have a glass of wine as an aperitif at La Madia di Giuseppe. Take the stairs to the restaurant. Enjoy the best of both worlds.

Ravioli di Ricotta e Spinaci con Pomodori Pachino e Basilico
Spinach and Ricotta Ravioli in a Cherry Tomato and Basil Sauce

There is always a choice of stuffed pastas at the Fornace di Mastro Giorgio, and this combination of spinach, ricotta, tomatoes and basil is a regular on the menu, either with conventional ravioli or mezzelune (half moon ravioli).

SERVES 4

Pasta:
200g plain flour
pinch salt
olive oil
2 eggs

Sauce:
olive oil
1 clove garlic, chopped
basil leaves
150g cherry tomatoes

Filling:
300g spinach
olive oil
pinch salt
1 clove garlic, chopped
150g Ricotta
2 egg yolks
50g Parmesan, grated
grated nutmeg (optional)

Mix all the pasta ingredients together and work them into a soft dough. Form into a ball, wrap and let rest. In the meantime, make the filling. Sauté the spinach with the oil, salt and garlic. Chop and mix with the ricotta, egg yolks, Parmesan and nutmeg, if using. Put to one side.

To make the sauce: sauté the garlic and a few basil leaves in the olive oil. Add the cherry tomatoes, season and let cook for a few minutes.

Roll out the dough as thinly as possible with a rolling pin or pasta machine. Cut into circles about 8 cm in diameter. Place a teaspoon of the filling in the centre of each circle, fold over the pasta and press the edges firmly.

Bring a large saucepan of salted water to the boil. Add the ravioli and cook for a few minutes until 'al dente'. Drain and serve with the sauce.

Wine suggestion: White – Cervaro della Sala di Antinori 2000, or Grechetto Vigna Tonda 2001 Antonelli

Piccione con Sformatino di Cipolla di Cannara e Salvia Fritta
Pigeon with an Onion Timbale and Fried Sage

Giuseppe loves pigeon dishes and Mirko's rendition with onion and sage is a particular favourite.

SERVES 4

150g onion, chopped
olive oil
1 whole garlic clove
1 bay leaf
stock
30g Parmesan, grated
2 egg yolks
100g double cream
butter and flour

breast and thighs from
  2 x 500g pigeons
olive oil, garlic, bay leaves
1 glass white wine

Garnish:
sage leaves, floured and deep fried

Preheat the oven to 170°C. To make the timbales: sauté the onion in olive oil with the garlic and bay leaf. Cook gently for 10 minutes with some stock if needed. Discard the garlic and bay leaf. Add the Parmesan, egg yolks and double cream and mix well. Butter and flour 4 moulds, pour in the mixture and cook in a bain-marie for 25–30 minutes.

In the meantime, cook the pigeon breasts and thighs in oil, garlic and bay leaves, ensuring that the inside is rare. Put the meat to one side and make a gravy with the meat juices, flour and wine.

Place the timbale and meat on a plate with the meat and pour over the gravy. Decorate with the floured and fried sage.

Wine suggestion: Red – Campogrande 1999 Lamborghini, or Sagrantino di Montefalco "25 anni" Caprai 2000

Montefalco

Known as the *ringhiera*, or balcony, of Umbria due to its high position and 360-degree views of the region, today Montefalco is synonymous with wine: Rosso di Montefalco and Sagrantino, to be precise. The lovely Piazza del Comune is unfortunately often used as a car park, but the town, which also boasts a number of interesting textile shops, is nevertheless well worth a visit.

L'Alchimista Cristina Magnini and Patrizia Moretti

L'Alchimista
Piazza del Comune 14
06036 Montefalco
T: + 39 0742 378 558
W: www.montefalcowines.com

Opening hours: 08.30 – midnight
Closed: Thurs evenings in winter
Holidays: 15 days in Feb
Covers: 30 inside; 50 on terrace

The story of L'Alchimista, like that of all alchemists, is about transformation. At the age of 22, having qualified as a sommelier, Cristina Magnini opened a small wine and food shop and convinced her mother Patrizia Moretti to join her.

But then, says Cristina, "an angel intervened" and they found a perfect position for a wine bar on the Piazza in Montefalco where a former art gallery became L'Alchimista. It was named after Patrizia who became, as she puts it, "the one in the kitchen who invents and transforms".

The menu gives customers an opportunity to taste the produce on sale in the shop. "The transformation of what we sell over the counter is another reason for the name l'Alchimista," says Patrizia. In practice, this means uncomplicated and reasonably priced food, although it's a long way from mere samples of ham and cheese. There's a tempting selection of salads, *bruschette*, Italian twists on brunch standards, such as scrambled eggs with truffles, and seasonal specials almost daily.

As word got around and the enterprise took off, Cristina convinced her father Claudio to leave his work in electromechanical assembly to help serve customers. By this time having asked two family members to risk their livelihoods she was getting a little nervous. However, less than two years since the frantic start-up, the venture is a resounding success – and it's still family-run. Even Cristina's little sister Barbara helps out when she's not studying.

It wasn't supposed to happen like this. As a qualified sommelier Cristina's original ambition was not to work with the family but only to work with wine. "It's so fascinating to read about and study, you want to keep going," she says.

That she is now doing so is, she freely admits, in large part down to her family's hard work. Not that it's always easy. As Cristina delicately puts it; "You

can be more direct than with other people, so …an extra word can come out." But, she adds, "we work very well together as we're all working for the same thing".

The mouth-watering array of goods on display is proof that they do work well together, not to mention the many elegant or personal touches: excellent and plentiful nibbles are served with aperitifs and there's a good choice of wine by the glass, as well as beer, coffee, chocolate and a selection of Patrizia's freshly baked cakes. There are even a few well-chosen quotes from Virginia Woolf and Manuel Vasquez Montalban on the inside cover of the menu.

This family mood is all part of the charming, gentle, laid-back feel of L'Alchimista, or as a local American resident and regular puts it, why would Cristina and her parents want to hire help from outside the family? It wouldn't be the same.

Certainly you'd have trouble finding someone who enjoys meeting people as much as Cristina does. Being a Montefalco native, she loves to know why so many people have come to her home town, and she will find out, not just in Italian but also in good French, better English and, one day she hopes, German.

So, two years on, how does Cristina feel about the success of her converted art gallery? "It started as a bit of a joke," she says. "We thought we could do something here, but I never thought it would become this big." And today? "Today my world is beautiful because there's always something new." Further proof, perhaps, of the transforming power of l'Alchimista.

Clockwise from above:
A superb spot on the Piazza in Montefalco was transformed from an art gallery into L'Alchimista.

Claudio, Cristina's father who was persuaded to join the family in their venture.

Patrizia, "the one in the kitchen who invents and transforms."

Barbara (in the background), Cristina's younger sister who helps out when not studying.

Cristina Magnini, sommelier and driving force behind L'Alchimista.

Insalata di Orzo Perlato
Pearl Barley Salad

One of Patrizia's most popular summer dishes, and very easy to throw together especially if you use tinned beans and chickpeas.

SERVES 6

200g borlotti beans
200g peas
200g chickpeas
500g pearl barley
stoned green and black olives
  to taste, sliced
small bundle of rocket,
  finely chopped

5 or 6 cherry tomatoes, cut into
  small pieces
pinch of salt and pepper
olive oil
balsamic vinegar

Cook the beans, peas and chickpeas. Boil the pearl barley in lightly salted water for about 20 minutes. Drain and leave under running water to cool.

Mix all the ingredients together. Dress with olive oil and balsamic vinegar to your taste.

Wine suggestion: White – Grechetto Barricato

Crostatina di Mele con Amaretti e Cioccolato
Apple, Amaretti and Chocolate Tartlets

A selection of fresh baking is offered daily at L'Alchimista. These tartlets are a year-round staple.

SERVES 8

Pastry:
3 eggs
180g sugar
10g butter
grated lemon rind
450g plain flour
8 level tsps baking powder

Filling:
4 amaretti biscuits, soaked in rum
2 dessert apples, peeled and
　cut into rough slices
choc chips as required
fruit jam

Preheat the oven to 180°C. Mix all the pastry ingredients together to obtain a soft paste. Roll out the pastry and put into 8 buttered and floured tartlet cases. Put a couple of teaspoons of jam, apple, crumbled amaretti and a few choc chips into each case. Put into the oven for 15–20 minutes.

Wine suggestion: Dessert – Sagrantino Passito

Norcia

Situated in the south-east corner of the region and neighboured by Monti Sibillini and the Piano Grande, Norcia is known for its pork butchers, truffles and Saint Benedict. The landscape in this part of the region is stunning.

Norcia has an industrious yet relaxed feel to it and, unsurprisingly, has some excellent food shops to browse around. Samples are abundantly handed out, and tasting encouraged. However, if you are tempted to buy home-bagged lentils from residents' doorways in nearby Castelluccio, be warned: they will probably require sifting to remove stones and grit.

Il Granaro del Monte
Carlo, Anna, Vincenzo and Federico Bianconi

Il Granaro del Monte
via Alfieri 12
Norcia
T: +39 0743 816 513
W: www.bianconi.com

Opening hours: 12.00 – 15.00
 and 19.00 – 22.30
Closed: open all week
Holidays: none
Covers: 250 inside;
 60 on outside terrace

Down a small pedestrian road, a truffle shaving away from Piazza San Benedetto, you'll find the Granaro del Monte restaurant. The restaurant is part of the Grotta Azzurra hotel, one of a group run by the Bianconi family. Its management is currently a joint effort between Carlo Bianconi, his wife Anna and their two sons, Vincenzo and Federico.

The Bianconi family has been serving food there through six generations. That's over 150 years. And still both locals and visitors to the area come here seeking Norcian specialities – and, even though there are seasonal changes to the menu, they always find them. Carlo explains: "Some things have been on the menu constantly for 50 years because they're expected here."

Everyone thinks of pork and truffles when they think of Norcia, he says. That may explain why fettucini with truffles is the most requested pasta dish in Granaro del Monte. In fact, "our customers won't eat *fettucini al tartufo nero* anywhere else; they want it here, no matter when in the year they visit".

But this is not a menu stuck in a time warp. Menu and food preparation have both kept pace with fashion and attitudes to nutrition. In his youth, says Carlo, food was full of taste but also full of fat; that was the way of things. It was also dictated by economics. When he was a boy his family owned pigs. An excellent way of making the most of them was *sanguinaccio*, a combination of pigs' blood, fat, orange and sugar that we know as black pudding. But the nutritional education of the clientele has brought about increasingly refined palates, a call for the reduction of fat and a renewed interest in vegetables. Now, by way of contrast, the more delicate combination of trout and courgette is offered. "Equally," says Carlo, "wild boar has had a resurgence in popularity; it's very tasty and a lot less fatty than pork."

However, centuries of sensitivity to customers' preferences also means that nothing is changed for the sake of it. The fire in one of the dining rooms has always been there and grilling is still done over real wood. In the kitchen "we don't start with pasta but with flour and eggs," says Carlo, adding: "The quality of our produce is fundamental; you can only elaborate something that is very good to start with."

The regulars at Granaro del Monte are a diverse bunch: obviously there are the locals who pop in frequently, but there are also many from much further afield. Every June a group of families comes from Bari, every May a group from London, and some Easter regulars have been turning up every year for 30 years. Nicole Kidman isn't a regular but she did drop in; she thought it was wonderful.

The next generation, Vincenzo and Federico, would agree. In fact, now in their early thirties, they have what at first sight appears to be a genetic commitment to the business. However, as Vincenzo tells it, his father ensured that they were not just passive victims of tradition. "When we were both teenagers he asked us what we thought about our professional future," he says. "He explained that if we didn't want to continue in the same line it wasn't a problem but in that case, he wouldn't invest heavily in it." Federico and Vincenzo talked about it all night. "In the morning we knew it was what we wanted to do," says Vincenzo. But first they both went off to university and spent time honing their language skills abroad

Clockwise from top left:
The terrace is sheltered and attracts both locals and visitors from much further afield.

The large kitchen runs like clockwork with all members of staff working hard and efficiently.

Vincenzo and Federico, the younger Bianconi generation, work closely together and turn an impromptu tasting into fun.

before bringing their own youthful ideas to the table. And now? "Here we are and we couldn't be happier." But also quite clear about the challenges. It's heavy work, they point out and can only be done with total dedication because, as Vincenzo notes, "it doesn't take up all your life – just most of it."

Vincenzo and Federico have nothing but admiration, not only for their parents' know-how but also their stamina and drive. "It's strange…sometimes our father seems younger than us," says Federico. However, Anna, Carlo's wife, seems to match his energy. She married into the Bianconi dynasty, and is the only woman in the family. She's also the family's strongest member. Ask anyone – or just watch her interacting with her men. However, it's not just her dedication but her warmth that is her strength – something the men don't always understand. "Sometimes we tell her that she talks to the guests too much and that she should leave them in peace," says Vincenzo. "A couple of minutes later 10 guests will arrive and tell us how fantastic she is and how wonderful it is that she stops to talk to them. Every time." And Anna? "She just looks at us. She knows she's right." And unstoppable. "Sometimes my brother and I pick her up and carry her to bed."

Carlo and Anna haven't set a retirement date, although they do recognise that the next generation will want their own space at some point. At least they know another Carlo is likely one day to run the place. It's a family tradition for the

Clockwise from above:
The fire in one of the dining rooms has always been there and grilling is still done over real wood.

Anna Bianconi, the "strongest member of the family".

Carlo, enthusiastically and energetically involved in every aspect of the business.

Federico, clear about how heavy the workload is, aware that he couldn't be happier doing anything else.

Vincenzo, who knew in his teens that this was the job for him, after university and time spent working abroad.

first-born son of each generation to be called Carlo and Vincenzo alternately.

The family ethos even permeates the staff, some of whom have worked here for 15 years. They eat together every day, members of a team putting in a vast amount of unseen effort to ensure that everything runs like clockwork and that the place retains its strong and loyal clientele. That's enough of an achievement, surely?

Not quite. Just listening to the current list of projects is exhausting. Tasting areas are planned, and cookery classes started recently, deliberately not run by 'super chefs' but by female traditional cooks taking small classes. There will also be displays of wine and cheese maturation, all organised to both educate and entertain. And there are numerous other gastronomic projects under way in the Hotels Posta and Salicone. But this isn't some sort of empire in the making. It is – and will remain – a large family enterprise with a small feel. The objective is to turn Granaro del Monte into "a very special gastronomic monument", says Vincenzo, although he probably knows that to many foodies it is already.

The Bianconi family is hard-working and ambitious, but also delightful, charming and a lot of fun. Every member cares deeply about every aspect of not only their business, but also, and most importantly, their customers. It's a great combination of enthusiastic individuals: Carlo is instinctive, Vincenzo and Federico are analytical – and Anna makes the decisions. Only joking, boys…

Above: All members of the Bianconi family are involved in every aspect of their business, from the start to the finishing touches.

Salsicce Farcite al Tartufo
Truffle-Stuffed Sausages

This recipe combines two of the culinary focal points of Norcia.

SERVES 2

6 fresh pork sausages
2 spoons chopped truffle
extra virgin olive oil
6 slices Norcian Caciotta
  (or another mild semi-soft
  cheese or porcini mushrooms)

6 slices wide pancetta or bacon
800g cooked greens (spinach,
  chard or chicory)
1 clove garlic
grated truffle (optional)

Preheat the oven to 180°C. Boil the sausages for 10 minutes, and put to one side to cool slightly. Season the truffle (black or 'scorzone' depending on the time of year) with the oil. Make a lengthwise cut in the middle of the sausage and put in a slice of cheese (porcini mushrooms work well as an alternative) and some truffles. Wrap up in the slice of pancetta. Put in the oven for 10 minutes to turn the pancetta golden.

In the meantime, sauté the greens with oil and a clove of garlic and put them in the centre of the plate. Arrange the sausages on top as soon as they are removed from the oven. If wanted, grate additional truffle over the top.

Wine suggestion: Full-bodied Red – Decugnano dei Barbi

Cinghiale in Salmi'
Wild Boar in Red Wine Sauce

Vincenzo explains that 'Salmi' is the term for a sauce that accompanies rich meat or game such as hare or pheasant. Red wine is used here (although completists should know that it can also involve marinating in blood…)

SERVES 4

500g lean wild boar
1 litre red wine
bundle of herbs (rosemary, sage,
  bay leaf, thyme and parsley)
1/2 carrot, cubed
1/2 stick celery, cubed
extra virgin olive oil
80g rosemary, sage, bayleaf, capers
  and garlic, all chopped

pinch bitter cocoa
ladle tomato sauce
50g black olives
salt
chilli pepper
1 litre meat stock

Cut the lean meat into cubes and put in a large bowl with the wine, bundled herbs and the cubed vegetables. Put the bowl in a cool place and leave to marinade overnight.

Drain the meat without discarding the marinade. Heat the oil in a pan, add the chopped herbs and the wild boar and brown for at least 15 minutes. Soften with the wine from the marinade. Leave on the hob, uncovered and when the wine has nearly evaporated, add the cocoa, tomato sauce, olives, salt, chilli and meat stock. Cook for at least 90 minutes. Serve with polenta.

Wine suggestion: Red – Sagrantino Adanti

Orvieto

Known, inevitably, for its white wine – Orvieto Classico – and striped cathedral, Orvieto is a delightful town that's got the balance between urban centre and tourist centre just right, as you'll see from careful observation of the Piazza del Popolo. At different times of day it's a quiet square, a car park or a bustling marketplace.

With a great number of artistic and historic gems, an above-average selection of shops and a significant *passeggiata*, it's easy to spend several

L'Antica Trattoria dell'Orso
Gabriele di Giandomenico and Ciro Cristiano

**L'Antica Trattoria dell'Orso
via della Misericordia 18 – 20
Orvieto
T: +39 0763 341 642**

Opening hours: 12.30 – 14.00
  and 19.30 – 22.00
Closed: Mon and Tues
Holidays: Feb and Jul,
  and 10 days in Nov
Covers: 60 inside. No outdoor
  seating but doors and windows
  open out onto square

Chef-proprietor Gabriele di Giandomenico has been running the Antica Tratto-ria dell'Orso for 23 years, although you'd never guess it to look at him; careworn he most certainly is not. Nor would you guess that he had earlier careers with James Bond's favourite gun manufacturer Beretta and then in the US fashion industry. He finally went back to Italy and Beretta but it wasn't the same. He was unhappy and told a cousin that he'd been cooking all his life and had often thought of opening a restaurant. So she bought one and told him to get on with it.

What she bought is rumoured to be the oldest dining venue in Orvieto. Its name harks back to the late 1800s when the Piazza was home to the local coal market with its accompanying bear *(orso)* show. The bear would be tied up right outside the existing trattoria.

Considering it wasn't entirely his own idea, Gabriele has done rather well. Situated off the beaten track just in front of Piazza Ascanio Vitozzi, the Trattoria dell'Orso inspires a fiercely loyal following among those who love simply pre-pared food served without pretension or stuffiness. And word about this relaxed, elegant restaurant has spread. Gabriele and partner Ciro have even attracted household names from the smart sets of Hollywood and London to their tiny trattoria.

Gabriele has his own way of doing things – and it is resolutely purist. " I have no secrets," he insists. "Nor", he adds, "do I have a freezer or a microwave". And he doesn't fry – or at least not very often. "If I fry something I throw away the oil, so I only fry a few very special things. If you want a fried cutlet, or fried pota-toes, this is not the restaurant for you." At night, whatever fresh ingredients have not been used are thrown away. "If you put food in the refrigerator it doesn't taste

Opposite above: Situated off the beaten track, l'Antica Trattoria dell'Orso's name harks back to the late 1800s and the bear show at the local coal market.

Opposite below: Gabriele (right) and Ciro (left) have worked together for 15 years, and "it's still fun".

the same any more," Gabriele says.

This approach is proof that Gabriele prefers to eat "with my mouth, not my eyes"; he resists fancy garnishes that add nothing to the taste of a dish and only uses plain white crockery. The point, he argues, is that if you can make a good dish of spaghetti with tomato sauce, you are a good cook. "Then again," he muses, "nobody really makes tomato sauce the way we make it."

This uncompromising allegiance to fresh, untainted food has a direct impact on the regulars, he suggests. "Their average age is a little bit higher than lots of other places, because we're not so cheap." Not so pricey, either, one might add, for the quality on offer.

Antica Trattoria dell'Orso is a small operation: Gabriele single-handedly takes care of everything in the kitchen, while Ciro quietly and charismatically looks after the tables. There is a menu posted on the door. Ignore it. Ciro will talk you through the choices, explaining perhaps that the mushrooms bought today are particularly good, and returning after the *primo* to go through the *secondo* options. Ciro may be co-owner but that's not why he's so attentive; he's driven by love of his work. "If you don't do this job enthusiastically, you'll never do it well," he insists.

How does Ciro find working with Gabriele? "Like all artists, he's a bit crazy, but we work very well together," he says. "We've worked together for nearly 15 years and it's still fun."

Professional respect between the pair is mutual: Ciro may hear the compliments paid to the food, but Gabriele is equally aware of how highly Ciro's warm welcome and professional service are regarded. In any case, he likes to come out of the kitchen for the occasional chat with the diners. They certainly enjoy it, not least because he has an endless fund of amusing, and frequently outrageous, stories, which, sadly, we have neither the room nor the courage to repeat here.

Gabriele is clearly fond of his customers and grateful for their loyalty but they do frustrate him in one respect. "I would love to do more things but they don't give me the chance," he complains. "Many of my regulars come for certain things and they know what they want before they arrive. The pasta with mushrooms is probably the most popular and lots of people are disappointed to find I haven't made the farro in the summer when it's 40°C!"

This loyalty manifests itself in some extraordinary ways. The husband of one devoted customer asked Gabriele and Ciro to cater for 30 guests at her 60th birthday in February 2005. He even paid for the transport, which is just as well because the party took place in Virginia in the US.

This trattoria is about even more than good food and loyal customers, however, although they would be recommendation enough. If Gabriele wasn't

Opposite: Gabriele di Giandomenico and Ciro Cristiano enjoy a morning chat with a friend passing by their restaurant.

running this trattoria, he would be an interior designer and his restaurant shows a man who knows his own style. Dell'Orso is not lavishly, but lovingly furnished: red varnished chairs in one room and green varnished ones in the other with lots of typical Orvietan craftwork in the form of wood and ceramics. The simple yellow tablecloths with white covers are evidence of both a relaxed style and atmosphere. There is ongoing and constant attention to detail: a platter of fresh fruit on display changes with the season: cherries, apricots, figs – whatever looks and tastes most beautiful at any given time. "The woodwork isn't perfect and it's old, so it needed to be dark, and yellow is my favourite colour, so I put it every-where," says Gabriele. "The artwork is from local artists," he adds. "There's no theme – just things I like."

It is, clearly, a good life. However, Gabriele has had many offers from the great and the good of London society to establish a restaurant there. Has he never been tempted to move? "No," he says briskly. "I'm weather-dependent. I need sun-shine and a nearby beach."

Above: There is a relaxed style to the lovingly furnished Trattoria dell'Orso with lots of typical Orvietan wooden craftwork.

Coniglio al Finocchio Selvatico
Rabbit with Wild Fennel

Fennel seeds are a popular Italian seasoning and work particularly well here.
Gabriele leaves the rabbit under running water for some time in order to purify it.
As a guideline, the colour of the meat should lighten considerably.

SERVES 6

1 rabbit cut into joints	small pot sour cream
olive oil	2 spoons fennel seed
1 onion, chopped	pinch fresh thyme
2 slices speck or bacon, chopped	1 tablespoon balsamic vinegar
1/2 bottle white wine	freshly grated lemon zest

Leave the rabbit in running water for at least 2 hours. Put in a pan on a moderate
heat and cover until water extracts and starts to boil. Discard this extracted
water. Add olive oil, the chopped onion and speck or bacon. Brown gently. Add
the white wine. Cover and let simmer on the lowest heat for 15–20 minutes so
that all the wine is absorbed.

In a separate pan put the sour cream, 2 glasses water, the fennel seeds and
the fresh thyme (you only need a little as it is very strong) and let it all heat
through gently. Stir in the balsamic vinegar. Pour this over the rabbit and let
simmer for 10 minutes.

Before serving grate over lemon zest. Serve with green vegetables.

Wine suggestion: White – Chardonnay or Cervaro della Sala

Parfait al Pistacchio e Rhum
Pistachio and Rum Parfait

Gabriele enjoys making desserts. This one is not only easy but can be prepared well in advance.

SERVES 10

100g shelled pistachios
6 egg yolks
6 spoons of sugar

¹/₂ glass rum
400ml whipping cream

Grind the pistachios.

Make a zabaglione with the yolks and sugar: whisk until they become a light yellow and double in volume. Add the rum and mix well. Whip the cream and fold in the zabaglione and pistachios. Divide between 10 individual ramekins or small bowls and put in the freezer for several hours.

Before serving, immerse the moulds in warm water to facilitate extraction. Garnish with seasonal fruit.

Wine suggestion: Dessert – Calcaia Barberani

L'Asino d'Oro Lucio Sforza

L'Asino d'Oro
vicolo del Popolo, 9
Orvieto
T: + 39 0763 344 406

Opening hours: 12.30 – 15.30;
 19.30 "till when I'm tired"
Closed: Mon
Holidays: mid–Jan to late Mar
 and mid–Oct to mid–Dec
Covers: 15 inside; 40 outside

Lucio Sforza is a true culinary original. He's also the owner and chef of a stylish, relaxed eatery with arguably the most attractive outside eating area in Orvieto. L'Asino d'Oro can be found along a cut-through linking Corso Cavour and Piazza del Popolo. Lucio found a warehouse here, at the end of a narrow alleyway that opens up into a delightful spot, and chose it for the site of his new trattoria when he was looking to downsize from his former larger establishment in Orvieto.

He had already established a huge reputation and following. So why move to a smaller site? Because, he says, the ego boost of running a vast restaurant year-round is no compensation for the loss of other things. Things like painting, reading, travelling and spending time with his children and grandchildren. In his smaller premises he works for seven months a year, focuses on his other interests for the remaining five and returns to his professional kitchen raring to go.

The décor at l'Asino d'Oro is calm and soothing. There's a big cabinet in the first dining room that was designed by Lucio based on recollections of a cabinet from his childhood. In the back dining room there are 1950s mirrors bought from an antiques dealer in London, although they are placed high on the wall to prevent an outbreak of narcissism distracting customers from the food or their fellow diners. Despite all these elegant old touches, the overriding impression of the place is one of modernity thanks to the gentle colours, plain wooden furniture, simple, functional water glasses and elegant wine glasses.

Does the food live up to the surroundings? Yes, it does. But then Lucio takes the research of his dishes and the preparation of them very seriously. "A region expresses itself through its dialect and its food," he insists. "So to enter into the

culture of a place you need to be able to speak or feel the language and eat the food." No ingredients are used that are out of season – or out of region. He will only use produce from the area and *territorio*: nothing comes from further than 20km away. This respect for *territorio* even extends beyond his own. He loves travel and submerges himself in the culture, tradition and mores of wherever he goes. "I can't listen to Jimi Hendrix in the Congo," he insists, "and equally I can't eat spaghetti in Berlin."

And his cooking? He enthuses about the 'cucina povera' that is part of his region's culture, delighting in the challenge of taking what was once peasant food and transforming it into something exquisite. That transformation has to be subtly handled of course. "A dish should be full of the flavours of the base ingredients. I don't want to transform a courgette into something else. A courgette should be a courgette." He will only use oil – not butter – to the point where even his béchamel is made with olive oil.

Assistance in the kitchen is ably and serenely provided by Flavia Lenarduzzi and Carmela Seretan, but Lucio retains responsibility for all dishes that leave this small but efficiently run hub ."I don't like to serve a dish that I haven't had some input into; I have to finish what's served." There's also the fact that Lucio obviously loves what he does. "This is my work, it makes me very happy and I really enjoy it. I especially like desserts because they're the fun bit. They're also important because the dessert is the last thing eaten and so it's remembered."

You can tell that Lucio chose his team, both in and out of the kitchen, with care. Just watch them at work. Unusually for a group of Italians there is minimal chatter – the job in hand takes priority. Watching the waiters prepare the dining room and terrace for lunchtime service – cleaning tables, laying out mats, cutlery and glasses – is poetry in motion, an extraordinary mixture of focus and relaxation. They're a good-looking bunch too.

Not that Lucio hides in the kitchen. As befits a man who is constantly on the search for intellectual stimulation, he sees his chats with diners as one of the day's highlights. "I was talking to somebody today about the century of the Renaissance and we started by discussing the food, and finished with Michelangelo and Raffaelo," he says. "It's a lot of fun."

It is, but there are few points worth knowing before you visit l'Asino d'Oro: Lucio's views on children and cappuccino for starters. Children are enthusiastically received (in fact, if you arrive with a group of children, their needs will be addressed first), but whatever those up to the age of 12 eat will not be put on the bill. "They don't usually eat very much and it's simply a gesture of courtesy," he says. And the cappuccino? Custom has it that cappuccino was traditionally only served in the morning, so don't bother asking for it. Lucio respects custom.

Opposite: L'Asino d'Oro is in a delightful spot, with arguably the most attractive outside eating area in Orvieto.

As you'll discover when you sample the menu. Try a *fuori pasto*. Lucio argues that antipasti are not Italian, but French, and that the correct tradition is to serve dishes that are 'outside', not 'before' the meal, and that were eaten at any time by workers in the fields. You might, however, prefer just a vegetable dish or dessert. There's no obligation to go through the whole menu, or indeed to have a complete meal.

You should also be aware of the fact that the menu is handwritten and is only in Italian, complete with notes where Lucio feels that an explanation would be beneficial. Don't worry if your Italian is far from fluent though. Any questions you offer in English will be answered helpfully by the glamorous Cinzia Maria Fusari or Enrico, who fully understand not only what l' Asino d'Oro is serving, but the rationale behind these choices.

Nor are foreigners treated with any less respect than locals. An American who eats here several times a year during her annual stay in Orvieto says she never has to remind Lucio that she's vegetarian. It's not just the food, she insists, but also the atmosphere, the feel of the place that matters. There is a presumption that the customers understand and care about food. "They know they're somewhere a bit different," Lucio says. "We're not looking for some perfect customer but they need

Above: Lucio retains responsibility for every dish that leaves his small but efficiently run kitchen and insists on having some input into everything that is served.

to be intelligent – we are closed to stupidity."

Lucio Sforza is a culinary original all right, although he simply describes himself as being "a bit mad", and trying to avoid doing the obvious. True enough. After all, how many other eating establishments are named after a comic novel written in the second century?

Mad he may be, but he was lucky enough to be at the front of the queue when talents in many areas were being allocated: he's an adventurous and gifted chef, an excellent manager and inspiration to his team, an accomplished painter, well-read, erudite, civilised, and has the courage of his convictions. Any flaws? Well, he's on his third marriage, but we're scraping the bottom of the baking dish here. The world needs more Signor Sforzas.

Above: Enrico serves Lucio's exquisite dishes to the diners outside. Fine weather means that places on the terrace at L'Asino d'Oro are sought after.

Following spread, left: The plain wooden furniture and simple, unfussy table settings give a modern feel.

Following spread, right: Cinzia Maria Fusari and all the waiting staff fully understand the rationale behind the choices on the menu.

Budino di Asparagi con Crema di Ceci
Asparagus Terrine with a Chickpea Cream

More often than not you'll find a 'budino' on Lucio Sforza's menu, which means that he offers an extensive variety depending on what is in season: courgettes and amaretti, peppers and plums or this one, which is a great way of using abundant asparagus.

SERVES 6

extra virgin olive oil
1 onion, chopped
1 stick celery, chopped
1 kg asparagus
marjoram
basil
50g pine nuts
gelatine sheets (approximately 10
  sheets, depending on gelatine used)

250g dried chickpeas
  (soaked and cooked)
1 lemon
extra virgin olive oil (approx 250ml)
parsley, chopped

Remove the woody part of the asparagus. Lightly fry the onion, taking care not to brown it. Add the celery, the asparagus, the marjoram and basil leaves and approximately 500ml of water. As soon as the asparagus is cooked, remove from the heat and add the pine nuts. Mix everything together, and put through a blender. Mix in the previously soaked gelatine sheets and pour into a greased baking tin or terrine dish. Leave to cool and put in the fridge to set.

Put the chickpeas in a blender with the lemon juice and slowly add the olive oil to form an emulsion. Keep in the fridge until ready to serve.

Slice the terrine and serve 3 medium slices per person on a bed of the chickpea cream with a drizzle of olive oil and a scattering of chopped parsley.

Wine suggestion: White – Orvieto Classico

Salsicce con l'Uva Passa Sausages with Raisins

This may seem unusual – and it is, but, as Lucio says, it is also very, very simple.
It is therefore essential that the pork sausages have to be top quality.

SERVES 6

handful of large raisins per person
Vin Santo
olive oil

12 pork sausages
flour as needed

Soak the raisins in Vin Santo for a few hours. Heat the olive oil in a pan and brown the sausages thoroughly. Add the raisins and Vin Santo to the sausages. Mix a bit of flour with some water and stir into the pan. Serve!

Wine suggestion: Dessert – Vin Santo or Sagrantino Passito

Le Grotte del Funaro Sandra Ricci

Le Grotte del Funaro
via Ripa Serancia 41
Orvieto
T: +39 0763 343276

Opening hours: 12.00 – 15.00
 and 19.00 – 24.00
Closed: Mon
Holidays: 10 days in Jul
 (dates vary)
Covers: 130 inside; 30 outside

If the name didn't give it away, you would probably guess. After a dramatic descent from street level down a large staircase, you really will find yourself eating in The Rope Makers' Caves. At least that was its primary purpose until nylon rendered rope making largely irrelevant and Sandra Ricci and her husband Alfredo established their restaurant on the site of the long-abandoned rope making works 23 years ago.

Not only Sandra and Alfredo's high standards but the need for state approval meant it took two years to convert the caves as they wanted. Sandra didn't mind. "It took a long time – but after all it is our heritage," she says. Their aim was to fit the restaurant harmoniously into the dramatic existing interior by going down the classic, as opposed to the modern, route. So traditional furnishings are scattered with more personal pieces, such as what Sandra describes as *la vecchia madia usava la mia nonna,* a chest for making and storing bread that her grandmother used. Also attractive are the range of wood-burning stoves you may pass on your way to be seated, but they're not just here for decoration: pizza is served in the evening.

The majority of the food, however, is classic Umbrian cuisine – and substantial portions of it. Sandra believes that several things contribute to her restaurant's success, but that it is essential to have good, fresh produce, something Umbria has in abundance. "We're very lucky to be in Umbria where the specialities are truffles, mushrooms, wild boar, pork and the like. *Noi facciamo i piatti tipici umbri che si basano sempre sui prodotti stagionali e soprattutto umbri,*" she insists. "We make typical Umbrian dishes always based on seasonal produce and Umbrian products." They also offer special menus for Easter, Christmas and the truffle period.

Not that there isn't a little market research on occasion. When new dishes are introduced, there's a month of testing involving all members of staff. It takes time of course because preferences are subjective. "Sometimes my husband and I disagree – *anche questo e normale!*" Nevertheless, they insist on getting it right. "More tomato or less tomato, more salt or less salt…and so on, until the dish is ready."

No detail is overlooked. "Good wine is very important," Sandra insists, "as are good oil, good cheese – and of course, good service. Fabrizzio is very important to us." That's Fabrizzio Grilli, who has been here over a decade and heads up the waiting staff. He could not be more helpful, especially when offering cheerful, professional and above all informative help with the bewilderingly long wine list.

The classic and dramatic aspects of Le Grotte del Funaro attract a mix of both regular locals and tourists. "Tourism is important to us in Orvieto" admits Sandra, "but we have a strong Italian base to our custom."

That's not too surprising. It's hard to pick a highlight from the menu, but the Chianina beef served here is amazingly tender and the pizza bread with a sprinkling of oil and rosemary is delicious to nibble on while choosing from the menu – or simply looking around at the old Etruscan tufa caverns. It may even briefly distract you from the excellent food and wine. Then again, where else will you find such a setting?

Above: Sandro and Alfredo took two years to transform the former rope makers' caves into their dramatic restaurant.

Zuppa di Farro all'Arrabbiata Spicy Farro Soup

"I adore soups", says Sandra. This hearty one nourishes and warms no matter how cold it is outside.

SERVES 4 – 6

200g farro	500g canned tomatoes, chopped
$^1/_2$ onion, chopped	salt and pepper
1 chilli pepper, finely chopped	extra virgin olive oil
1 litre stock or water	

Soak the farro for 4 hours. Lightly fry the onion and chilli, add the soaked and drained farro. Mix in half the stock and simmer for 40 minutes. Add the tomatoes, the rest of the stock, salt and pepper and cook for a further 20 minutes. Farro absorbs a lot of liquid so extra stock may be required.

Serve very hot with a generous drizzle of extra virgin olive oil.

Wine suggestion: White – Grechetto Umbria Barrique, Cantina Barberani

Ombrichelle del Funaro Funaro Pasta

Porcini mushrooms feature heavily in the menu at Grotte del Funaro, and this is the restaurant's signature pasta dish. Ombrichelle are long, round, thick strands of pasta made from flour and water only, and are a local speciality.

SERVES 4

1 clove garlic, chopped
olive oil
4 fresh or preserved porcini
  mushrooms
1 sausage

250g canned tomatoes, chopped
400g ombrichelle pasta
  (or tagliatelle)
parsley, chopped

In a frying pan, lightly fry the garlic in the olive oil. Cut the mushrooms and sausage into small cubes and mix in. Leave to cook for about 5 minutes. Mix in the tomatoes and cook for a further 10 minutes. In the meantime, cook the pasta in salted water. When the pasta is cooked mix in everything and sauté in the pan for a few seconds.

Serve on a plate garnished with chopped parsley.

Wine suggestion: White – Castagnolo Cantina Barberani

Perugia

The region's capital, Perugia is a vibrant city with a youthful buzz, due in no small part to its thousands of students. The Umbria Jazz festival is a big draw in July, as is the Chocolate Festival in October. On a more sedate note, the region's main art gallery is here and there are some beautiful parks strung along the edge of the city.

The Perugian *passeggiata* down Corso Vannucci, ending with a linger in Piazza IV Novembre, is a must.

Osteria del Gambero
Angelo Zarbo and Marco Casavecchia

Osteria del Gambero
via Baldeschi 17
Perugia
T: +39 075 573 5461

Opening hours: 19.30 – 23.00,
  and 12.30 – 14.30 (Sun only)
Closed: Mon
Holidays: Jan and Aug
  for two weeks each
Covers: 45

Angelo Zarbo and Marco Casavecchia: the men who control the day-to-day running of Osteria del Gambero. What a double act.

Angelo, the chef, a Sicilian who settled in Umbria with his young family after 17 years in Germany, is ambitious, driven, inventive, enthusiastic and thrilled to be in a region full of the high-quality primary produce from which he makes his living.

Marco, the head waiter, a local man, who loves Italian coffee ("it's what I really miss when I go abroad. It's not as good anywhere else"), hates shopping and endures a lot of good-natured abuse about his taste in clothes, is so laid-back that he appears to be offering his, always pertinent, advice from a horizontal position.

The two men complement each other brilliantly. But they're not quite the star turn of Osteria del Gambero. That, inarguably, is the food, which is why many consider it to be the best restaurant in Perugia, although Angelo has a more than modest influence on this assessment.

Angelo, like many a chef from his region, is inspired by the sea. He's delighted that, in the past few years, Umbrian resistance to fish-eating has begun to break down, as is Aulon Sulaj, his young Sicilian sous-chef. It may of course have something to do with the two unbelievably good-value menus – one fish, the other meat – on offer at the restaurant, although those are not the only culinary attractions. There's also excellent bread, baked in-house daily, with rosemary, nuts or onions and sage. The cheese selection, meanwhile, is taken very seriously indeed, so much so that there's a separate cheese menu.

It's all superlative food – and at a more than a reasonable price. Guglielmo Gamberini, the owner, explains that he wanted to "establish a restaurant that wasn't luxurious, but that served great wine and interesting food without being

Opposite: The restaurant's modest location in an unprepossessing side street does scant justice to the culinary delights on offer inside.

stuffy or pricey". He describes his restaurant, with evident pride, as "beautiful, elegant, offering creative, innovative food". That is down to Angelo who changes his base menu seasonally and his specials daily. He too is proud that people find things here that they just won't find elsewhere, and is aware that even though being situated in Perugia means that there's passing tourist trade, "we count on the regulars who live here to give us our good name".

Which they do, clearly aware that Angelo Zarbo serves up a great variety of inspired dishes, cooked with consummate skill. In fact, under the guidance of its chef, Osteria del Gambero is a bit of culinary heaven in the region's capital.

The restaurant is situated in a small, unprepossessing side street. However, once in the back room at Osteria del Gambero, you have a splendid view over the rooftops of Perugia and surrounding countryside. There's also a marvellous diversity of clientele. For all the linen, beautiful, large white crockery and glasses, Osteria del Gambero attracts a varied crowd, the young, trendy and casually attired sitting next to the more senior suits and posh frocks.

So, is there a secret to the restaurant's success? Angelo and Marco both laugh. "No, there's no secret" replies Marco. "It's work, hard, hard work" stresses Angelo. *"C'e la passione* and a drive to convey that passion" adds Marco. "The whole team is important, because the chef by himself is nothing." They're right: it is work; it is passion; it is the people. But it's above all the sublime food.

Opposite: Angelo Zarbo, creating inspired dishes with consummate skill.

Above: The back room at Osteria del Gambero provides a splendid view over the rooftops and surrounding countryside of Perugia.

Coda di Rospo farcita con Gambero in Foglia di Spinaci su Vellutata di Zafferano
Monkfish stuffed with Spinach Wrapped Prawns on a Saffron Velvet

A typical Angelo fish recipe; beautiful to look at – and delicious too.

SERVES 4

1 kg monkfish (2 tails)
8 large prawns (2 pp; 1 for the
   stuffing and 1 for the garnish)
150g spinach leaves
1 strand saffron

1 glass fish stock
100ml fresh cream
extra virgin olive oil
salt and pepper

Preheat the oven to 170°C. Parboil the prawns and cool in iced water. Cook the spinach leaves and put to one side. Clean the monkfish tails, remove the backbone and any skin. Extract the two fillets from each, open them out, flatten with a meat tenderiser and sprinkle with salt and pepper. Shell half the prawns and wrap in spinach leaves. Arrange the prawns in the centre of the monkfish, roll up and tie with kitchen twine. Cook in the oven for about 20 minutes. Prepare the saffron velvet by adding the saffron to the fish stock, reducing until quite thick, and stirring in the cream.

Put the saffron velvet in the centre of the plate, slice the monkfish into rounds about 2cm thick and add over the sauce. Finish the plate with a stream of olive oil, and garnish with an unshelled prawn.

Wine suggestion: White – Chardonnay Planeta

Filetto Farcito con Tartufo e Caciotta in Salsa di Sagrantino
Beef Fillet stuffed with Truffles and Caciotta in a Sagrantino Sauce

A great combination of Umbrian specialities and a wonderful recipe to make if you've returned home with, or have to hand, some black truffles, Caciotta and Sagrantino. If not, some inventive substitution will still result in a fine dish.

SERVES 4

800 g beef fillet (200g pp)
black truffle from Norcia (150g fresh, sliced or 50g of truffle paste)
200g Caciotta (or a soft cheese such as a Bel Paese or Fontina)
8 slices pancetta, or streaky bacon (2 slices per fillet)
string
250ml Sagrantino wine
extra virgin olive oil
salt
knob of butter

Cut each fillet horizontally, but not quite all the way through, and open as a book. Stuff the fillet with slices of truffle and Caciotta. Wrap the pancetta around the edge of the fillet and bind it with kitchen string. Lightly fry it on both sides in the olive oil for about 2 minutes, and then add the Sagrantino wine to the pan. Check the seasoning, and keep on a high heat to reduce the amount of liquid and thereby intensify the flavour. Remove from the heat and bind the sauce with a cold knob of butter. Serve immediately.

Wine suggestion: Red – Campoleone Lamborghini – Umbria

La Piazzetta
Riccardo Parparelle and Vittorio di Vittorio

La Piazzetta
via Deliziosa 3
Perugia
T: +39 075 573 6012

Opening hours: 12.00–15.00
 and 19.00 – 23.00
Closed: Tues from the end of
 Oct to Easter
Holidays: no set dates
Covers: 125 inside; 22 outside

La Piazzetta's owners are keen to point out that they offer traditional dishes revisited in a modern context. Their restaurant, by contrast, brings the modern into the traditional.

The restaurant has only been around for some 20 years, but the building which La Piazzetta now occupies was once a refectory for priests. In fact parts of the building go even further back. The structure was built during the Renaissance, but on old Etruscan walls rumoured to be the old city walls of Perugia itself.

La Piazzetta has been open for business since 1982, but present owners Riccardo Parparelle and Vittorio di Vittorio took over a couple of years ago. Neither of them claim any professional experience of cooking. In fact they are more than happy to keep out of the kitchen and let the experts get on with it – most of the time. Both, however, care about good food, and let their chefs know it. As Vittorio puts it: "We study what they do, we suggest, we try, we amend, we discuss their suggested recipes and then we choose the final dishes that go on the menu."

It's a menu that changes almost every other month. "Our dishes are new, fresh and innovative – and always with seasonal produce," Vittorio explains. "The changes come from my own experience, what I see as I travel around."

Generally, though, they both concentrate on what they know and like best: looking after customers. "That's why we have so many regulars. We never leave the dining room in the hands of others; we look after everything that leaves the kitchen and everything that goes on in the dining room," says Vittorio.

Like many young Italians, Riccardo first waited tables while he was a student. Unlike most of them, however, he liked it so much that it became his life's work. For co-proprietor Vittorio the route was less direct. He, like Riccardo,

Opposite: The menu at La Piazzetta changes regularly to include new, fresh and innovative dishes.

worked in hotels and restaurants while studying in Perugia. However, although he too had discovered his future passion, his agriculture degree took him to work in various control functions on the agrarian and agricultural side of the EC. After ten years of this, the work, and more specifically the constant moving around the country, lost any appeal it may once have had. What he wanted was a job he could enjoy and which allowed him to stay put. He found it in his former life in the restaurant business and in teaming up with Riccardo.

The clientele at La Piazzetta is predominantly local, regular and reliable, a priority for Riccardo and Vittorio, who are wary of trimming or compromising to attract the notoriously unpredictable tourist market. However, a fair number of tourists do find the restaurant during the town's busy period, a period which extends from Easter through summer until the annual week-long October Chocolate festival, Eurochocolate Perugia, which is a major attraction.

Before the next Eurochocolate, however, there's work to be done. Although the two owners are clearly proud of the old structure and setting of the restaurant, that doesn't mean they don't have plans. The long unused wine cellar is about to be put into service, with wine stored by the cask and sold on a retail basis. You can't stand still in this business. Even if you are standing within fifth century walls.

Sformatino di Ricotta con Funghi Porcini e Tartufo Nero
Baked Ricotta with Porcini Mushrooms and Black Truffle

A dish using three favourite Italian ingredients.

SERVES 4

200g Ricotta	**rosemary**
salt and pepper	**1 garlic clove, crushed**
60g Parmesan	**extra virgin olive oil**
2 egg whites, beaten	**black truffle**
handful Porcini mushrooms	**bread, toasted and cut into soldiers**
bayleaf	

Preheat the oven to 180°C. Mix together the ricotta, salt, pepper, Parmesan and egg whites. Sauté the mushrooms in a frying pan with the bayleaf, rosemary, garlic and extra virgin olive oil.

Take 4 individual aluminium moulds, put a spoon of the mushroom mixture at the bottom and fill the rest of the mould with the ricotta mixture. Cook in a bain-marie in the oven for about 45 minutes.

Once cooked, reverse the mould onto a serving platter and grate over the truffle. Serve with the toasted bread brushed with extra virgin olive oil.

Wine suggestion: White – Chardonnay Barrique I.G.T. "Colli Perugini"

Risotto con Porcini, Foie Gras e Salame d'Oca
Porcini Mushroom Risotto with Foie Gras and Goose Salami

A very rich risotto, which is a popular choice at La Piazzetta.

SERVES 4

1 medium onion, chopped
300g risotto rice
2 bay leaves
olive oil
¹/₂ glass white wine
1 litre meat or vegetable stock
130g goose salami, diced into small, even pieces

70g cooked foie gras, diced
200g fresh mushrooms (ideally porcini), roughly chopped
rosemary
1 clove garlic, chopped
100g Parmesan

Heat the stock and keep simmering on the hob. Sauté the mushrooms in a pan with a bay leaf, rosemary, garlic and oil. Season.

Sweat the onion gently for 5 minutes in some olive oil. Add the rice to the pan and mix thoroughly into the oil and onion until every grain looks glossy. Add one bay leaf and the wine. As the wine evaporates, add the hot stock ladle by ladle, stirring continuously, letting the liquid be absorbed before adding the next ladle. Halfway through cooking add ²/₃ of the goose salami, ²/₃ of the foie gras and the porcini mushrooms.

The risotto may not take all the stock; it's ready when the grains are plump but with bite in them. Serve with the remaining salami, foie gras and Parmesan.

Wine suggestion: Red – Rubesco D.O.C. "Cantine Napolini"

La Bottega del Vino

La Bottega del Vino
via del Sole, 1
06122 Perugia
T: +39 075 571 6181
W: www.labottegadelvino.net

Opening hours: 12.00 – 15.00
 and 19.00 – 24.00
Closed: Sun

A wide selection of Umbrian and Italian, and an eclectic choice of foreign wines let you know that La Bottega del Vino is not some run-of-the-mill watering hole.

Situated on a first floor overlooking Piazza Danti, and a fabulously cool escape from the summer heat, the bar is especially popular during the Umbrian Jazz festival. The staff are all knowledgeable, helpful and unobtrusive. Great for a light lunch, but essential for an aperitif or after-dinner drink, this is a gem of a place.

Caffe Sandri

Caffe Sandri
corso Vannucci 32
(diagonallly opposite the
National Gallery of Art)
T: +39 075 572 4112

Opening hours: 08.00 – 22.00
Closed: Mon

This wonderful café and pastry shop has been on the Corso Vannucci since 1860; the current owner is from the fourth generation of the founding family.

You can sit outside, but do wander in to see the vaulted, frescoed ceiling and lavish array of sumptuous, home-made confectionery. For a sugar fix with that espresso, just point to the slabs of chocolate: milk (*al latte*), cappuccino (*bianco con il caffe*) and plain (*fondente*) and say how much you'd like weighed out.

Pigge/Trevi

Pigge is approximately 4km outside Trevi, which stands proudly –
and dramatically – above the Via Flaminia. Trevi is a labyrinthine
interconnection of streets clinging onto the hillside, although it also
has some interesting museums. There's even a Museum of Olive Oil,
which is not as odd a concept as it sounds. The area has long been
famous for the quality of its oil, which derives from the characteristics
of the soil in which the olives are grown.

La Taverna del Pescatore
Catia and Claudio Menichelli

La Taverna del Pescatore
via Chiesa Tonda 50
Pigge
Trevi
T: +39 0742 780 920
W: www.latavernadel
   pescatore.com

Opening hours: 13.00 – 14.30
  and 19.30 – 21.30
Closed: Wed
Holidays: varies from year
  to year
Covers: 30 inside; 60 outside

Some of the restaurant owners in this book might, if pushed, suggest that they are pleased to have found attractive establishments near sources of good produce. Claudio Menichelli, however, goes a little further. For him, the position of La Taverna del Pescatore, at the meeting point of two valleys, evokes the culture of the Valnerina, the monastic experience of Saint Benedict, water, earth, livestock, Montefalco wine, Trevi olives and a whole lot more.

"The Etruscans, the Romans, the Carthaginians, the great travellers of central Europe, explorers – every person has been enchanted by this area," he says. "This is a meeting place of both wine and gastronomy, a concentration of the culture of the north and north-east of Italy, as well as the culture of the south of Umbria. Right here. *E un posto magico.* It's a magical place."

Phew. He also has strong opinions about traditional Umbrian cooking. There isn't any. Or at least, not as we understand it. It's important, he insists, to know the difference between *vera tradizione o tradizione per turisti* (true traditions and the traditions for tourists), pointing to such variables as the seasons, the elements and ancient history as inspirations for the eel, monkfish, crayfish – once a local native and now imported – sea bass, turbot and other fish he serves. The Menichelli family also bought a plot of land a few years ago, land now used for their own olive oil production, because, he says, "oil is fundamental and the olive is a symbol of peace and antiquity".

La Taverna del Pescatore is largely a family affair. There are six members, supported by extra staff: Claudio's son and daughter, his mother, who makes the pasta and prepares the vegetables, his father, who looks after the pork, mushrooms, asparagus and truffles, and of course his wife Catia, the chef.

One wonders whether the family's involvement is also part of what he feels makes the restaurant magical. "It's truly beautiful," he says, but before you get carried away with the idea that this too is somehow part of his interest in the spiritual dimension of place and tradition, he makes it clear that no one who works in his restaurant gets a free ride. "My children and all my family have been trained: both my children have professional sommelier qualifications and they've done courses on chocolate distillation and on cheeses. My wife teaches cooking and has taught in Hong Kong and in Sydney."

Rushing around her kitchen at an extraordinary speed, Catia Menichelli cuts a slight but energetic and commanding figure, confidently in charge of her culinary kingdom and daily-changing menu, albeit one with a fixed structure: soup, antipasto salad, stuffed pasta and then three main fish and three main meat courses.

Her bustling style is in stark contrast with the quiet, restful surroundings of the restaurant on the banks of the River Clitunno, a short way from the Via Flaminia. The location started life as a fisherman's house in 1919, became a restaurant in 1964 and was acquired by the Menichellis in 1990.

La Taverna del Pescatore is off the beaten track, but that's why finding it is so rewarding. With a small bridge leading to an island, it's an oasis of calm. On coming upon it, the Menichellis had the feeling that they had somehow found themselves in the middle of a Claude Monet painting. It's hardly surprising that, in addition to the regular staff, even more have to be hired during summer to cope with demand when the setting is at its most achingly beautiful.

Compared to the animated and effervescent Catia, waiter Mirko Angeli is calm and relaxed, albeit he is one of the most helpful and affable of waiters, for whom nothing is too much trouble. Hailing from Sant'Eraclio, just outside Foligno, he came to Taverna del Pescatore after a stint at Villa Roncalli. He's proud that the restaurant refers to its diners as guests not customers, and that the service aspect is important. "It's our pleasure to serve people," he states with total sincerity.

In his spare time, Mirko delights in being a hunter-gatherer, sourcing food from its starting point. It's a family tradition: he gets together with his father and grandfather to eat sausages and go hunting, fishing, or foraging for wild mushrooms and wild asparagus. "It's important for me to be out in nature; this passion has been handed down from generation to generation in my family."

One suspects Claudio approves of this enthusiasm for nature and history. The inspiration for the restaurant, he says, comes from "the study of our farmers and artisans of our earth; the artistic, historic and cultural spirit of our people." Not that inspiration alone is sufficient. "Yes, it's magical, but that means we have to be strong and raise ourselves to the height of this place because we can't feel comfortable here without producing something extraordinary." Don't worry Claudio, you do.

Clockwise from top left:
The restaurant is found on the banks of the River Clitunno.

Catia Menichelli cuts a slight but energetic and commanding figure in her kitchen.

In the summer, the long terrace along the riverbank comes into its own and the whole setting is at its most achingly beautiful.

Even a shot of caffeine cannot remove the feeling of calm that pervades La Taverna del Pescatore.

Schiacciatina di Patate di Colfiorito con Tegame di Gamberi di Fiume
Crushed Colfiorito Potatoes with Pan-Fried Crayfish

A popular dish at the Taverna del Pescatore. Although Catia uses Colfiorito potatoes and Trevi olive oil, any good mashing potato and extra virgin oil will fit the bill.

SERVES 4

400g red Colfiorito potatoes (red and waxy)	**salt**
600g live crayfish	**black pepper**
chives	**extra virgin Trevi oil**
sage	**wine vinegar**
1 clove garlic, crushed	**tarragon**
	parsley

Boil the potatoes in salted water, then peel and mash them with a fork. Season with chopped chives, sage, garlic, salt, black pepper, oil and a drop of wine vinegar.

Boil the crayfish in a small amount of water, then shell and separate the head from the tail. Put the tails in a pan with olive oil, finely chopped tarragon and parsley, salt and pepper. Heat gently for a few minutes until the herb flavours have been absorbed, taking care not to overcook the fish.

Arrange the potatoes centrally on the plate and scatter the prawn tails over the top and garnish with the boiled heads. Finish off with a drizzle of Trevi extra virgin olive oil and parsley.

Wine suggestion: White – Colli Martani Grechetto Grecante, Caprai

Bocconcini di Capitone ad uso dei Pescatori
Fisherman's Eel

Catia kills, cleans and skins her eels herself for this dish. You, however, might prefer to delegate that part to your fishmonger.

SERVES 4

1 eel (approx 1 kg)	20g capers
olive oil	rosemary
1 garlic clove	half a bayleaf
1 carrot, grated	wild fennel
1 celery stick, finely sliced	150ml vegetable stock
1 leek, finely sliced	1 tomato, peeled, seeded and diced
1 shallot, chopped	

Clean the eel, remove the skin and cut into bite-sized pieces. Heat the olive oil in a pan and lightly fry the garlic, carrot, celery, leek, shallot, capers, rosemary, half bay leaf and wild fennel. Add the eel and stock to the pan and cook gently, bathing the fish continually with the stock. Season. When almost cooked add the tomato and remove from the heat.

Serve with the vegetables in the centre of the plate and the eel placed on top.

Wine suggestion: Rosé – Rosa del Golfo

Scheggino

The small village of Scheggino is a sleepy, peaceful place, many of whose residents can be seen sitting on benches watching the world go quietly by. The morning regulars in the cafe are all known and don't even need to order their 'usual'. Occasionally visitors pass through, often taking a break from walking in the Nera valley. You can, however, see a reminder of a more turbulent past in the famous 12th century walls that held off the bandit Girolamo Brancaleoni in 1522.

Del Ponte Rita Strappato and Marco Ronca

Del Ponte
via di Borgo 15
Scheggino
T: +39 0743 61253

Opening hours: 12.00 – 14.30
  and 19.30 – 22.00
Closed: Mon
Holidays: 15 days in Nov
  (dates vary)
Covers: 130 inside and 40
  in the garden

Among the specialities of the Del Ponte restaurant 90 years ago was lamb with black truffles. That dish was cooked by Rita Strappato's grandmother, the first of three generations of the same family to work in the Del Ponte kitchen.

Rita was cooking with her mother and learning the family's cooking techniques when she was a child; many of the traditional dishes and cooking techniques she was taught remain in her repertoire. However, since she took over at Del Ponte in 1990 after five years at hotel school, there have been a few adjustments. Much of the past generation's reliance on butter, lard and heavy fats has given way to the use of extra virgin olive oil, a sign, says her husband Marco of the times. Marco, who heads up the waiting staff, and has worked at Del Ponte for 15 years, points out: "It's to be expected that the clientele will change over the years. Customers have become more demanding; they expect more easily digestible food."

That doesn't make it any less delicious of course. Home-made tagliolini with black truffles, which has featured on the menu since the early days, is particularly good and the most requested dish. However, there is no shortage of demand for more recent innovations, like homemade *tagliolini di farro*, made with farro flour, which Rita describes as "darker than the usual pasta; it looks a little like wholewheat".

The farro is sourced from nearby Spoleto. Rita and Marco try to source all their primary materials locally from suppliers who can be relied upon to meet their demanding standards of quality. The meat too is local, "from small farms, good quality meat, reared properly," says Rita. And the reliance on only local ingredients doesn't stop there. The grilled lamb on the bone, for instance, is particularly sweet here, and that's not just because of the quality of the meat. As

Marco explains: "We choose local wood especially for the grill; this is very important for the taste."

The diners at Del Ponte are equally split between locals and passing trade. Alongside regulars from the surrounding area who return every weekend you will often find tourists on walking or trekking holidays in this beautiful and idyllic part of Umbria. The concealed, shady terrace is particularly popular in the summer, while indoors the decor retains the local feel. Having said which, the owners do like to give it an annual makeover. "We try to get things that say something about this area," says Marco, pointing to the paintings decorating the dining room. "These pictures are from a local artist here in Scheggino, although he's quite famous and now lives in Perugia."

It's a combination of tradition, quality and carefully managed change that has kept Del Ponte going for close on a century. And in case you were wondering, the lamb with black truffles is still on the menu. It has to be; it's Rita's favourite dish.

Above: Husband and wife, Rita Strappato and Marco Ronca.

Opposite: The waterside location of Del Ponte is a real draw, especially to walkers in the summer.

Insalata di Farro al Tartufo
Farro and Truffle Salad

One of the most popular starters at Del Ponte and another recipe that combines Umbrian favourites, in this case farro, truffles and pork sausages.

SERVES 10

500g farro
200g pork sausage
200g peas
300g porcini mushrooms, sliced
500g champignon mushrooms, sliced
300g cream

Black Truffle Sauce:
50g butter
2 spoons stock
100g black truffles, chopped
truffle to grate

Simmer the farro for about an hour. Drain and leave to rest. In the meantime, heat some oil in a pan, add the crumbled sausage, peas and mushrooms. Adjust the seasoning and leave to cook for 10 minutes. Remove from the heat and mix together with the previously cooked farro and the cream. Put to one side and make the truffle sauce by melting the butter together with the stock and mixing in the chopped truffles. Gently heat and put two spoons of the sauce on top of the farro at the moment of serving. Grate truffle over the top.

Wine suggestion: Red – Ciliegiolo Colli Amerini

Trota ai Ferri e Spiedino di Gamberi
Grilled Trout with Crayfish Kebabs

A simple and easy way to prepare fresh fish, this recipe can also be adapted for barbecue cooking in the summer.

SERVES 10
10 trout
200g breadcrumbs
small bunch of parsley,
  finely chopped
juice of 1 lemon
oil as needed
salt to taste

Kebabs:
50 crayfish
10 skewers
lemon, sliced for garnish

Prepare the breadcrumbs in the same way for both the trout and crayfish: put them in a bowl and add the lemon juice, parsley, salt and oil, and mix well so that the ingredients are thoroughly combined. In the meantime clean and fillet the trout and stuff the fish with the breadcrumb mixture.

Clean the crayfish and season with salt, pepper and partially coat with the breadcrumbs. Brush the trout with oil, and grill, checking from time to time to see if more oil is needed. The trout should require about 15 minutes of grilling. In the meantime put 5 crayfish on each skewer and grill, but for only 8 minutes. The trout and skewer of crayfish should be served together with a slice of lemon.

Wine suggestion: White – Grechetto de l'Umbria

Spello

Spello is a charming hill town, rising up to overlook the Valle Umbra. Very easy to navigate, as it's long and thin, the main road links the two main gates, Porta Consolare and Porta dell'Arce. Off this main artery are many narrow and cobbled side streets. There are excellent views from the Belvedere and some delightful and fascinating shops.

La Bastiglia Marco Gubbiotti

La Bastiglia
via dei Molini
Spello
T: +39 0742 651 277
W: www.labastiglia.com

Opening hours: 13.00 – 14.30
 and 20.00 – 22.00
Closed: all day Wed, and Thurs
 lunchtime
Holidays: Jan 7–20
 (but dates can vary)
Covers: 50 à la carte;
 120 for organised events

At the top of the main thoroughfare that runs through the delightful hill town of Spello, the terrace of the restaurant at La Bastiglia has a sweeping view over the lush Umbrian countryside. But that's not why everybody in the know raves about the restaurant. That's down to Marco Gubbiotti, his team and the food they produce. Since receiving a Michelin star at the end of 2004 however, Marco's irresistible food is the worst-kept secret, even among those without their finger on the gastronomic pulse of the region.

La Bastiglia offers an upmarket and sophisticated menu served in a serene environment. Overseeing it all is chef Marco Gubbiotti. He is an intense and dedicated man, but no tyrant; he doesn't need to be. There is a potency to the calmness in his kitchen that signifies a well-managed team in which every member knows exactly what they should be doing and when.

Marco spends a lot of time researching and reflecting upon the dishes he plans to introduce to each season's new menu, reaching for his notebook during spare moments at work – or even in the middle of the night – to ensure nothing is overlooked, although "sometimes I rebel and introduce some new dishes mid-season," he adds with a grin.

Marco spent five years training at college, but sees his education as an ongoing process. Although he comes from Spoleto, he has travelled a great deal, working for four years at Villa Roncalli in Foligno and completing training sessions in Paris and Siena "and still I keep researching. *Io sono alla continua ricerca della cucina di territorio.* I'm constantly researching. I have lots of old recipe books of central Italian cookery."

Although the starting point for his recipes is the region's cooking – local

Opposite above: The restaurant is a huge draw for local, and not so local, residents.

Opposite below: The terrace of La Bastiglia, with its sweeping view over the lush Umbrian countryside is popular with diners in the summer.

products and recipes from generations ago, he uses this as the foundation to build his own recipes, combining his imagination with the modern preference for lighter, more easily digestible food, ably aided by his hard-working and efficient sous-chef Andrea Santilli.

This fascination with, and respect for, the past combined with his willingness to embrace new techniques leads to some intriguing experiments. "Can I find the scent and flavour of a particular dish, say home-cooked roast chicken with garlic and roast potatoes?" he asks. "Can I find that and put it inside stuffed pasta? It's the search for these things that interests me."

Another modern innovation is a vegetarian menu – but this is not some menu of token variations on stuffed peppers, as its popularity with both Italians and non-Italians attests. How about *strangozzi* in asparagus and pea sauce with a pesto of wild herbs and matured ricotta? Or a celeriac pancake with a verdant selection of fresh herbs and Taggiasche olives? Marco loves cooking vegetables and thoroughly investigates cultivation techniques, especially those of farmers who grow crops in the most natural way possible. Incidentally, the popularity of the vegetarian menu is such that it is by no means assumed that diners are actually vegetarians. If you don't eat meat, let your waiter know that your preference extends to the pre-dining nibbles.

Not only is Marco's cooking flawless but he has an extraordinary gift for the visual. Everything, from the beautiful glass bread 'basket', which features a mix of home-made grissini and seeded brown and white breads, to plates which feature mosaics of colour and are elegantly composed, underlines the kitchen's attention to the harmony of every dish and the overall rhythm of the complete meal.

This attention to quality permeates the entire restaurant. Since Marco's arrival at La Bastiglia in 1998 there's been a steady stream of improvements – and not only on the food front. The seating has been upgraded, the tablecloths are linen, the cutlery silver and the glasses crystal. Food, surroundings – in fact everything, from the warm, friendly atmosphere that greets you when you enter to the perfectly composed plate of treats that accompanies coffee – reflects Marco's belief that all aspects of the dining experience are important.

And the popularity of the restaurant proves his point. Obviously many of the diners are guests in the hotel, but it's also a huge draw for local, and not so local, residents. There are frequently large tables of Italian family or work gatherings, gesticulating animatedly and tucking in with gusto.

They'll no doubt be glad to hear that Marco's travelling days are over – for a while at least. "I'm very happy here. It's peaceful, it's very green and I love going out in the morning to pick my herbs."

Opposite above: Marco Gubbiotti, Michelin-starred chef of La Bastiglia.

Opposite below: Pasta is made on a daily basis and Marco's willingness to experiment leads to some unusual, but successful combinations.

Frittelle di Baccala con Guazzetto di Sedano, Foie Gras, Pere e Borragine
Salt Cod fritters with Celery, Foie Gras, Pears and Borage

Truly delicious to cook yourself, though Marco takes this dish to heights even the best of us can only dream of. If they're on the menu when you visit La Bastiglia, they are not to be missed.

SERVES 6

For the fritters:
300g soaked salt cod (soak the salt cod in cold water for 24–36 hours, refreshing the water several times)
oil
chilli, chopped finely
1 garlic clove, crushed
50g onion
rosemary
280g milk
80g flour
1 egg
level teaspoon bicarb of soda

For the guazzetto:
300g celery
50g pork cheek or pancetta in one piece
clove of garlic, whole
oil

1 litre extra virgin olive oil for frying
150g foie gras
2 Abate or Williams pears (if the latter, need to be slightly underripe)
20g icing sugar
50g borage

To prepare the garnish: halve the pears vertically and then cut a total of 12 slices about 2mm thick at their largest part (a mandoline is useful here). Keep the remaining fruit. Spread the slices out on a sheet of greaseproof paper on a baking tray, dust with icing sugar and put in the oven at 80°C for about 2 hours.

Cut the foie gras into small cubes and put in the freezer. Cut the remaining pear into cubes of the same size and put to one side in water and lemon.

To prepare the fritters: remove the skin and bones from the salt cod and cut the fish into small pieces. Heat the oil, chilli, garlic, onion and rosemary and add the salt cod, followed by 200g of the milk. Make a paper cover and heat gently without boiling (the paper cover will help to ensure that the temperature remains uniform and that it doesn't boil). Simmer for about 15 minutes, or until the cod breaks apart when pushed gently with a spoon. Drain, remove the rosemary, and either beat finely with a knife or put into a food processor, to end up with a paste.

To prepare the guazzetto: remove stringy bits from the celery, keep the best bits to one side for the garnish and finely slice the rest. Heat the oil, the pork cheek and garlic. Mix in the celery and cook for a few minutes. Discard the pork and garlic and keep the celery to one side.

Separately prepare the batter with the remaining 80g of milk, flour and egg. Mix in the salt cod and the bicarb of soda.

Shape the salt cod mixture with two dessert spoons and add orange peel to the oil. Heat the oil and fry the fritters until golden. Assemble on a plate with the cubes of foie gras and pear, the pear slices, celery strips and borage

Wine suggestion: White – Cervaro della Sala 95, Soave la Rocca Pieropana 98

Controfiletto di Chianina Steccato con Lardo Stagionato, Salsa di Sagrantino, Pomodori e Radicchio Secche

Seasoned Lard-Studded Sirloin of Chianina with Sagrantino Sauce, Tomatoes and Dry Radicchio

If you're lucky enough to be able to get hold of Chianina beef this is a marvellous way to prepare it. However, you should get excellent results from most top-quality beef.

SERVES 4

12 ripe cherry tomatoes

extra virgin olive oil

salt and pepper

2 Trevigiano radicchio
 (long, not round, radicchio)

2 Chianina beef sirloin steaks,
 about 700g each

50g of seasoned lard, sliced finely,
 or streaky bacon

string

30g shallots, finely chopped

sage and rosemary

fresh garlic clove, chopped

600ml Sagrantino

aromatic seasoning (sea salt flakes,
 wild fennel, sage, rosemary, lemon
 peel – all chopped together)

freshly milled pepper

Cut the tomatoes in half horizontally, remove the seeds, sprinkle with oil and salt and put in a 140°C oven for 1 ¹/₂ hours. Cut the radicchio into 4 lengthwise, sprinkle with oil and salt and put in the oven at 140°C for about 2 hours.

Remove the fat from the meat and cut 2 medallions of about 3 cm high from each steak. Cut each steak to about halfway through in the direction of the meat fibres. Put the slices of lard into these cuts and secure by tying the string around twice. For the Sagrantino sauce, put the shallots, oil, herbs and garlic into a small pan and fry gently. Mix in the wine and reduce until it becomes syrupy. Strain, cool and keep to one side.

Brown all sides of the meat in a very hot frying pan and then put in a preheated 200°C oven for 5 minutes. Remove and let it rest for about 2 minutes in a warm place. Serve it sliced in half, this time in the opposite direction to the original incisions (against the meat fibres), ie all the way through, horizontally through the earlier cuts. Add the aromatic seasoning and fresh pepper, pipe a line of the reduced Sagrantino and arrange the tomatoes and radicchio to serve.

Wine suggestion: Red – Sagrantino di Montefalco 25 anni 1995 Caprai or Cepparello 1997 Isole e Olena

La Cantina Fausto Benedetti

La Cantina
via Cavour 2
Spello
T: +39 0742 651 775

Opening hours: 12.30 – 14.30
 and 19.30 – 22.00
Closed: Wed
Holidays: none
Covers: 60

There has been food served on the site of La Cantina for over 25 years. Its vaults, however, are a little older, dating from approximately 1200, when it was the cellar (*cantina*) of a country house. Fausto Benedetti, the present owner and chef, arrived a decade after paying guests first entered the establishment. When he took over it was a pizzeria. He, however, had other ideas.

Originally from Foligno, he has impressive culinary contacts there: Marialuisa Scolastra of Villa Roncalli is his cousin, and Salvatore of Il Bacco Felice is an old friend. Like them, he had a vision, and so the pizzeria became a restaurant – a restaurant where he could offer simple cooking of high-quality food.

Like its owner, La Cantina is calm and sedate. It's a feeling that permeates Fausto's restaurant, even in summer when, although there is no outside eating area, large paddle fans keep the diners cool.

And there are quite a few of them; La Cantina has an enthusiastic local following. The regulars return not only because they know that the basic produce will be sourced with care but also because the finished product is reliable.

The key is simplicity. Fausto especially likes cooking grilled meat and does so over an open fire, with only minimal additions. "One of our great local products is olive oil and a few drops of that on grilled meat is a fine dish," he says. Hence his observation that the popularity of his restaurant is inextricably linked to the quality of the produce he uses because his cooking is very simple.

Simple, but always effective. Although Fausto changes his menu seasonally, some items are always featured when at their best: truffles, *porcini* and Chianina beef. Like all the meats chosen so diligently, Fausto likes to cook the latter simply – on the grill. After all, he says, "the grill can't obscure anything. If the meat is good, it shows."

Opposite above: La Cantina is situated a few steps from the Piazza della Repubblica, and its vaults date from approximately 1200 when it was the cellar of a country house.

Opposite below: Fausto Benedetti prepares simply cooked, high-quality food for an enthusiastic local clientele.

Crostini con Pate di Melanzane
Aubergine Pate Crostini

Although Fausto serves this as an antipasto it's also good as party and picnic food.

SERVES 4

1 large aubergine
salt
half a crushed garlic clove
heaped teaspoon of capers
dried oregano

extra virgin olive oil
tomatoes, skinned, deseeded and
 chopped
12 small slices of bread

Preheat the oven to 180°C. Put in the whole aubergine (as it is, no oil or seasoning) for about 20 minutes. Remove from the oven with care, as it will be hot. Remove the skin. Chop the flesh and put into a bowl with the salt, garlic, capers, oregano and oil. Blend everything together (with a mixer attachment).

Toast 3 half slices of bread per person and spread on the aubergine cream. Garnish with the tomatoes.

Wine suggestion: White – Grechetto

Orecchiette con un Pesto di Rucola
Orecchiette with a Rocket Pesto

This uses a lot of rocket, but mixing rocket and watercress works just as well.

SERVES 4

500g rocket	**olive oil**
2 basil leaves	**salt**
pine nuts as needed (approx 3 tbsp)	**400g orecchiette**
1 clove garlic	**Grated Parmesan**

Bring a pan of salted water to the boil. Add the rocket. When the water returns to the boil, remove from the heat and drain. Leave to cool.

Put the cooled rocket into a blender with the basil leaves, the pine nuts, garlic, olive oil, some salt. Whizz to make the pesto. Remove the pesto from the blender and pass through a sieve to remove the tough stalks.

Cook the pasta and then mix in the pesto sauce thoroughly. Sprinkle over freshly grated Parmesan and serve.

Wine suggestion: Light Red, or a White Grechetto

Spoleto

The 750ft Ponte delle Torre aqueduct, the Duomo, the fortress Rocca Albornoz and the Roman amphitheatre remain Spoleto attractions, but it was opera composer Giancarlo Menotti and his Festival of Two Worlds that put Spoleto on the modern map. Running for three weeks from mid-June to mid-July, it attracts visitors from all around the world.

L'Osteria del Matto Filippo Proietti

Osteria del Matto
vicolo del Mercato 3
Spoleto
T: +39 0743 225 506

Open: 13.00–15.00 and
18.30 (for drinks);
20.00 – 22.30 (for dinner);
22.30 – 02.00 (for drinks)
Closed: Tues
Holidays: usually 3 weeks in Aug
Covers: 25, and 16 on the terrace
in summer

Filippo Proietti has barely opened his mouth before he mentions two overriding themes of his osteria: good, simple food and the family. Referring to the local pasta dish *Strangozzi alla Spoletina*, he explains: "My Mamma puts the pasta in water, starts the sauce, and when the pasta is ready the sauce is ready".

The parental reference is not entirely surprising. Eating at Osteria del Matto is a bit like eating with a friendly and generous family, which, in a sense, you are. To begin with you're positively encouraged to relax, to browse through books and CDs on the shelves if you wish. More to the point, everybody gets the same food.

There is a good reason for this. The set menu at both lunch and dinner, is based on that morning's available produce. It's important for Filippo that the raw ingredients are fresh and seasonal, although when availability is limited that may mean an equally limited menu. Diners never worry, however. Mamma will do it justice.

She uses whatever her son brings back from the market, cooking by experience and instinct, using her eye for food and her taste for quality, as her mother did before her, rather than the dictatorship of a recipe book. And the results are more than agreeable, although being responsible for everything in a kitchen where one day five and the next day 10 different dishes may be required is no mean task. Pasta, farro, prosciutto, cheese, potato slices in sesame seeds – the list is at the mercy of local suppliers, but always cooked with a touch of inspiration. Alessia, Filippo's sister, recently started working with her mother in the kitchen and learning the family's culinary secrets because this continuation is important.

As Filippo is keen to underline: "This is family work." In fact family was what made the Osteria del Matto possible in the first place. Hailing from Spoleto, Filippo spent a year working at an Oxford college, followed by a few years

Opposite: The Osteria del Matto, situated just off Spoleto's market square was a disused laundry when Filippo acquired it.

working in Edinburgh for the family of Giancarlo Menotti, the founder of the Spoleto Festival of Two Worlds. Returning to Spoleto in 1999 with a dream of opening his own restaurant, he found the place he was looking for. It was positioned in a small exit from Spoleto's market square, Piazza del Mercato. At the time, however, it was also a disused laundry.

No matter. He invested his life's savings and the inheritance from his grandmother in buying the, somewhat dilapidated, premises, and spent the following year fixing it up. It reopened as the Osteria del Matto on 20 December 2000 with his mother in the kitchen and his father helping to serve.

The family feeling translates to the osteria itself, a small establishment, catering for only 25 people inside, at shared tables if necessary. Does Filippo wish to expand the restaurant? "No. I aim to speak to everybody who comes here and make them feel truly welcome, so I need to have time to answer questions on the cheese or explain the sourcing of the ham. If I cater to more guests, that will no longer be possible."

It also won't be possible for Filippo to use his social engineering skills in positioning his guests, either alone ("I can usually tell when people wish to sit quietly in the corner by themselves") or, more often, with others. "I try to put people together in a positive way so that they can enjoy the experience of sharing a table," he says. And he usually gets it right. "Sometimes people decide to meet up the following day because they've had such a nice time together here."

Clockwise from above:
There is a general feeling that a fabulous time will be had most evenings, and the wide choice of wine undoubtedly helps the evenings along.

Filippo was given his nickname "il matto", "the madman", whilst at school and it's obvious why it stuck.

Mamma uses whatever her son brings back from market, cooking by experience and instinct to produce an inspired menu.

Filippo brought a Pinocchio from home as decoration, and now has about 35 of them, all different and all presents from clients.

The nice time even extends to helping Filippo decorate. When he first opened the osteria, he put a Pinocchio from home on the wall. Some friends then gave him another one as a good luck present and these have turned into a collection of about 35 Pinocchios, all different and all sent from clients. "Sometimes people come in with a Pinocchio and swap it for a bottle of wine," he says, adding, with a slightly demented laugh: "I'm thinking of pinning a Eur500 note on the wall so that customers help me to collect euros as well."

Filippo clearly has a huge amount of affection for his customers. The feeling is mutual. "I love people to enjoy themselves here. Sometimes I feel a bit down, but then a present arrives from someone in New Zealand or Australia who came here once, a CD that they think I'll like for instance, and it gives me a real buzz."

A real buzz is what evenings at the Osteria del Matto are all about. The sign above the entrance exhorts visitors *Entra solo se bevi vino* (Enter only if you drink wine) and there is a general feeling that a fabulously sociable, if slightly unhinged, time will be had most evenings – and few people are as unhinged as Filippo. Hence, perhaps, the name of the Osteria, based on Filippo's nickname "il matto", "the madman". He was given it at school and you only have to meet him to see why it stuck: it's the name by which he and his restaurant are known throughout not

Above: Mamma takes a quiet moment in the morning to make strangozzi, a local pasta.

just Spoleto but the whole of Umbria.

Of course, the wide choice of wine undoubtedly helps the evenings along. Filippo's cellar has grown over the years to a more than respectable size, and he's always happy to make recommendations based on your preferences and budget.

The lunchtime crowd is a touch more subdued but as loyal as the evening diners and drinkers. Three of the most regular visitors are women in their mid-eighties, all ex-Red Cross, all widows, but still willing, and more than able, to spend two and a half hours eating and drinking with Filippo.

The Osteria del Matto is not flashy. It is, however, somewhere that you can be sure of simple, fresh food, packed with flavour at an incredible price. And beautifully cooked by Mamma. In the four years she's been working in her son's osteria, Mamma has lost 18kg, and a fair amount of sleep, but none of her desire to do justice to the fresh food her son supplies. That, after all, is what the locals flock here for – and why it's wise to book in advance.

You will also have a good time. Filippo "il matto" insists on it. "I have no wish to work in a factory where I simply process people. I like diners to leave having enjoyed themselves and speaking well of this osteria. That just won't happen if I don't try to make everyone feel special."

Above: Filippo is happy that people hold both him and his osteria in such affection, constantly reflecting on how to make all his guests feel both comfortable and special.

Strangozzi alla spoletina Spoleto Strangozzi

A recipe handed down through Mamma's family for generations, this has its origins as peasant food; in fact it's traditionally eaten with bread so that nothing goes to waste. Mamma feels strongly that quantities are irrelevant here: the cook should use whatever is to hand and be guided by personal preference. As for the making of the strangozzi, it's true that you should add an egg to the strangozzi with, say, a mushroom or truffle sauce ("so that the sauce and pasta come together on your fork", as Filippo puts it), but the strangozzi for this dish is made from just flour and water. As a simple guideline, the difference between strangozzi and tagliatelle is that the former is thick pasta, cut finely, and the latter is thin pasta, cut widely. Incidentally, Filippo is adamant that this should never, ever, be eaten with Parmesan.

SERVES 2

strangozzi (or tagliatelle) pasta
olive oil
garlic, chopped
parsley, chopped

ripe tomatoes (remove the skins
by pouring on boiling water and
then squeeze to get rid of the main
seeds, but do not totally deseed)
chilli pepper (optional)

Put the pasta on to cook. In a frying pan lightly fry the garlic and parsley in the olive oil. Turn the heat up to high and add the tomatoes, and chilli pepper if using. When the pasta is ready, mix everything together. Do NOT add cheese.

Wine suggestion: Red – Montefalco Rosso or Rosso di Lago Trasimeno

Crescionda

This is again based on a peasant dish where nothing is wasted, so if you have less than the required 350g of Amaretti biscuits, make up the weight difference with whatever leftover biscuits are to hand (but not so much as to obscure the flavour of almonds). Mamma serves this by itself, but Filippo has been known to serve it with double or clotted cream on visits to the UK.

SERVES 20

10 eggs

1 litre full fat milk

strong coffee (a mug with 4–5 tablespoons –not teaspoons– instant coffee)

12 tablespoons sugar

3 tablespoons cocoa powder

1 espresso cup mistral liqueur, or rum

350g amaretti biscuits

1 spoon olive oil, and extra for greasing

Preheat the oven to 200°C. Make the strong instant coffee and leave to cool.

Mix 2 spoons of sugar with the cocoa (in order to break up the cocoa granules). Slowly mix in a few spoons of the milk, and when smooth add the remaining milk.

In a separate bowl beat the eggs. Add 10 spoons sugar (1 spoon of sugar per egg) and beat again. Add the liqueur and beat in. Ensure that the coffee is cool enough not to scramble the eggs, and add. Roughly crush the biscuits through a mouli and stir into the liquid with a spoon of olive oil. Add the cocoa and milk mixture to this bowl, and mix thoroughly.

Grease a baking dish very well with olive oil and pour the mixture into it. Put into the preheated oven for about 20 minutes. It is done when the top darkens and becomes slightly crispy. Leave to cool and sprinkle with icing sugar before serving.

Wine suggestion: Dessert – Vin Santo

Il Panciolle Sandro Argilli and Luca Sbrenna

Il Panciolle
vicolo degli Eroli 1
(off via del Duomo)
Spoleto
T: +39 0743 45598
W: www.ristoranteilpanciolle
 spoleto.com

Opening hours: 12.30 – 14.30
 and 19.30 – 22.30
Closed: Wed in winter (Oct to
 May, depending on weather)
Holidays: two weeks, usually
 in Nov (dates vary)
Covers: inside 45; outside 100

Sandro Argilli and Luca Sbrenna played football together in their teens. Now Sandro runs Il Panciolle and Luca heads up the service side of the restaurant. And in between? Sandro worked all around Italy, came back to work in Spoleto and met and married Merella Nori, inviting Luca and his wife to be witnesses. Finally, after 20 years of working for others, he decided that he wanted to set up his own venture, and so, in March 1997, he and Merella bought Il Panciolle, with Merella as head chef. Luca joined two years later.

Sandro has some very specific ideas about certain aspects of his restaurant: combining the beautiful with the practical, for instance. The tablecloths are as elegant as they are functional, coming from Bergamo, a major centre of Italian textile production, where they are made by hand. The colours green and yellow are everywhere. Are they functional too? In a way. They happen to be his favourite colours but also, he insists, "they respect the internal ambience and they give luminosity, an Umbrian, Romanesque atmosphere".

He also believes that a certain amount of inventiveness is essential in a professional kitchen, notwithstanding the fact that *"noi facciamo una cucina che e legata al territorio umbro e piu specificamente spoletino."* Yes, he agrees that the food is part of the territorio, which is Umbrian, and more specifically Spoletino. But, he adds, he and his staff do research, taking their cue from the typical products grown in a given season, so the recipes become their own creations. "If you maintain that you are part of the culinary art then you can't just follow existing recipes. You need to create your own, paint your own gastronomic pictures." As Merella evidently does; his wife's passion for cooking is, he says, in her blood.

The menu changes 11 times a year, sometimes radically, sometimes with the

Opposite: The terrace of Il Panciolle gives a broad view over the rooftops and surrounding countryside of Spoleto and is a fabulous spot.

Above: Sandro Argilli, who runs Il Panciolle and who feels strongly that inventiveness is essential in a professional kitchen.

merest tweak. But in every change, the kitchen and the dining room staff are involved, not least in assessing the right wines for each dish. You can be sure of a good choice of wine, not only by the bottle but by the glass; wine is treated with the utmost seriousness here. As of course is food. Even the bread selection is unusually tempting – white and brown breads jostle for space with olive and walnut breads – and there's a marvellous choice of Italian cheeses. And yes, the cheeses are only Italian. Sandro and Merella will happily tell you why. "Italy has some extraordinary cheeses that France can only dream about."

And then there is Luca. Luca is one of the friendliest yet most professional waiters you are likely to come across. He has worked in England and is married to an Englishwoman, but is nevertheless more than happy to let diners practice their (sometimes very elementary) Italian on him, or, if he's unsure as to whether people wish to proceed in Italian or English, to ask pleasantly rather than score linguistic points. Either way he is delighted when diners want to discuss the food and wine that is served – and at Il Panciolle they usually do.

The standard of questions asked by the diners who make up the majority of the clientele is, Luca and Sandro insist, indicative of the discerning and knowledgeable visitors the restaurant attracts. But it's not an exclusive place. The

clientele is mixed: along with visitors to the town you'll see large Italian family groups, business meetings and a significant array of the young and beautiful from Spoleto.

The icing on the cake (if that's not an inappropriate phrase) is a fabulous terrace with a broad view over the rooftops and surrounding countryside of Spoleto. Luca says he feels that both the serving staff and the diners feel more freedom in every sense when they're on *la terrazza panoramica*. It's especially popular in the summer when the loud birdsong on a warm evening adds an extra dimension to the dining experience.

In Panciolle means the art of chilling out, of relaxing. The setting, food and service all combine to make that pretty easy. Free language lessons from Luca included with your meal.

Above: Luca Sbrenna is one of the friendliest yet most professional waiters you are likely to come across.

Bruschette Miste alla Spoletina Mixed Bruschette

Merella offers this platter of different bruschette. Although they complement each other, any one of these is good enough to be served on its own.

Take 4 slices of good quality, dry white bread per person and toast lightly. (Merella always does this over a fire).

Garlic:
1 garlic clove pp

Take the toasted bread, grind over sea salt, pour on extra virgin olive oil (both to taste) and then put a peeled garlic clove on a toothpick and serve upright on the bread, so that diners can rub the clove over the toast to the desired extent without tarnishing their fingers.

Tomato:
Chop the required quantity of vine tomatoes, deseed and leave in a sieve for about 10 minutes, so that any excess water runs away. Mix with salt and oil and add herbs if wanted. Spoon the tomatoes on to the toast and garnish with a basil leaf.

Chicken liver:

300g chicken livers, finely chopped	**rosemary**
1 large glass wine	**1 small onion, finely chopped**
scant 1/2 glass white wine vinegar	**1 celery stick, finely chopped**
1 glass olive oil	**piece lemon peel**
1 clove garlic, finely chopped	**anchovies and capers to taste**
sage	

Put everything in a pan on a very low heat. Merella feels that the domestic cook should add in whatever other flavourful meats are to hand, for instance leftover salami, prosciutto or sausages. The liquid should cover the meat; add extra if necessary. Season if required. Put on a very low heat, and cook gently for about an hour until the liquid has disappeared. Put through a blender and mix thoroughly.

Cover the toasted bread evenly with the chicken liver paste.

Truffle:

200g black Spoleto truffles

2 cloves of garlic, whole

30g butter

3 spoons of extra virgin olive oil

2 small anchovies

the juice of a lemon

2 anchovies, crushed

Carefully clean the truffles with a medium-hard brush, checking that no stones or clots of earth remain.

Put the garlic and oil in a pan and fry for a few seconds. Remove the pan from the heat, discard the garlic and add salt and pepper. Mix the butter into the hot oil and when the oil has cooled grate the truffle into it. ("Heat doesn't do truffles any good," explains Merella). Blend well and mix in the lemon juice and anchovies.

Spread on to the toasted bread.

Wine suggestion: Rosé – Scalabrone di Antinori (Sangiovese Rosato)

Garganelli di Ragu di Agnello con Zafferano e Finocchio Selvatico
Garganelli Pasta with Lamb, Saffron and Wild Fennel

An alternative to garganelli is a short pasta such as penne or maccheroncini.

SERVES 4

300g lamb	wild fennel seeds
juice 1 large lemon	1/2 glass dry Marsala
1 small onion	375g garganelli
olive oil	pinch saffron
salt and pepper	knob of butter
rosemary, chopped	grated Parmesan

Mince the lamb and put it into a bowl of cold water and lemon juice (this softens and reduces the fat of slightly older lamb and removes the strong taste). Leave the meat in the water and lemon juice for the time that it takes you to finish mincing it. Drain the meat and put in a saucepan. Cook over a gentle heat and drain away the first extract of liquid. Chop the onion and fry in olive oil in a separate pan. Once the onion has softened, add the minced meat. Brown everything slightly, season and add the rosemary and the wild fennel seeds. Mix thoroughly. Add the Marsala and cook for 15–20 minutes for it to evaporate. In the meantime, cook the pasta with a pinch of saffron.

When the sauce and the pasta are ready, put a knob of butter in a new pan and mix the pasta and sauce together. Serve with the grated Parmesan.

Wine suggestion: Full-bodied White or young Red – Cervaro della sala Castello della Sala Antinori (white) or Montefalco Rosso Antonelli (red)

Terni

Terni is not an obvious holiday destination, despite being the second largest Umbrian town after Perugia. That, however, is a good reason to visit.

It has some beautiful areas, an unforced charm, and with its absence of tourists is the perfect antidote to hill town fatigue. It's also home to a Roman amphitheatre, lies a few kilometres from the tomb of Saint Valentine and the Cascate delle Marmore, Europe's highest waterfalls. These are worth a look (if they've been turned on; they're man-made, so check the timetable). Or just stroll along the mainly pedestrian thoroughfare, Corso Cornelio Tacito, where elegant locals shop and catch up on the latest gossip.

L'Oste della Mal'Ora Renzo Franceschini

Oste della Mal'Ora
via Tre Archi 5
Terni
T: +39 0744 406 683
W: www.ostedellamalora.it

Open: 18.00 till late
Closed: Sun
Holidays: Jul and Aug,
Christmas, New Year and Easter
Covers: 28

Renzo Franceschini's osteria is not an easy place to find – even when you're right next to it. If you spot the unassuming exterior and go in, you find yourself in a narrow space. That, in turn, leads into a small back room. Finding that room, however, won't do you much good at lunchtime; l'Oste della Mal'Ora is only open in the evenings.

So why make the effort? For three very good reasons. Because the owner really knows his wine. Because the food is excellent. And because it's always fun. People don't come here just to eat and drink, but for social interaction: it's almost impossible to remain uninvolved, not only in your neighbours' conversations, but in the banter of diners and drinkers three tables away, many of them medical staff who work nearby ("it's our favourite part of the hospital", as one of the regulars puts it). Occasionally one of the dermatologists arrives with his guitar. You'll probably also spot a few architects, lawyers and the occasional professional footballer having a swift one before an early night. Well, swiftish…

This had been an enclosed storeroom for many years until in 1998 Renzo chose the space for a project ancillary to his core wine business. That business is a thriving and full-time concern, and Renzo is a serious player in the Italian wine industry, both as an expert and an entrepreneur. He is the founder of Vinarius, the association for Italian wine bars, and has been recognised in competitions and award ceremonies as one of Italy's finest sommeliers.

So what is Renzo trying to do? He explains: "In our osteria, we seek to recreate the spirit that was still alive in these types of places in the 1950s. Osterie then were neither restaurants nor trattorie, but places where people came with their own food already cooked and the owner gave them shelter from the elements (the

Opposite above: Andrea, Renzo and Beppe greet a regular at the Oste.

Opposite below: Renzo Franceschini, a fine sommelier and an excellent host.

origin of the word 'cover'), and offered wine, bread and products such as cheese and cured pork meats."

Even now people occasionally arrive at Oste della Mal'Ora with home-cooked food. Paolo, for instance, a radiologist and a great cook, frequently turns up with his speciality, a fish and mussel stew, which everyone shares. If, however, you plan to eat from the house menu you'll find a wide and mouth-watering selection of predominantly cold dishes and, on Thursday, oysters.

Renzo continues: "Every 'paese' had at least one typical local product and we have tried to collect the best from the rich Italian gastronomic panorama. So, depending on what's in season, we'll serve goat's cheese from a small producer in Pinerolo (Piemonte), who is a true cheese craftsman; salted anchovies from Lampedusa which are rich and meaty or a plate of different types of goose inspired by ancient Venetian traditions." A varied and wide-ranging selection, but, as Renzo puts it; "It's in the DNA of Italians to cook and eat well. We've grown up with certain culinary traditions."

As for the wine, don't worry, you're in the hands of experts. Choose a series of dishes with a certain theme and a few suitable bottles will be suggested. Or opt for a variety of different foods – a platter of mixed smoked fish, a rice salad, goose

Above: "It's in the DNA of Italians to cook and eat well. We've grown up with certain culinary traditions."

salami, a cheese selection and the *tagliere del cioccolato* (a big slab of chocolate cut into slices on a board) – and an appropriate wine will be served for each course, after, in all likelihood, an accompanying commentary from fellow guests on which you should choose.

Beppe, a neurophysician and regular, explains that Renzo "feels that many bottles of wine are becoming too expensive for daily consumption, so he actively searches out good, but reasonably priced ones, so that regulars can indulge each day without overspending". The majority of diners take full advantage of this philanthropic approach and go for a variety of choices by the glass, enjoying the moderately priced wine with a couple of courses, and then splashing out on a glass of something superb.

Andrea Barbaccia has worked in the Oste for several years now, but he started out as a regular customer. In those days he was managing another venue, but when Renzo invited him to work there he jumped at the chance. And he fits right in with the relaxed atmosphere. He's cultured, well-read, chats with everybody, regular or first-timer, and, despite the many distractions, always serves the right food to the right tables. He also speaks excellent English.

Fun and creativity are the watchwords of the Oste, but don't take my word

Above: The owner really knows his wine and actively searches out good, but reasonably priced ones.

for it; just read the house magazine. *Il Gazzettino dell'Osteria* comes out, its banner claims, when people are sober enough to produce it. You'll need excellent Italian, and a fair knowledge of Italian history, culture and current affairs, to get most of the jokes, but Beppe will happily talk you through a selection of his favourite articles. He's in residence Tuesdays, Wednesdays and Thursdays of most weeks.

Which just about sums up the Oste. It's not *Cheers* exactly; there's no insiders' clique. The intellectual curiosity and enthusiasm of the regulars ensures that they will want to talk to you, explain the menu and suggest wines for you to try. The food is superb, the choice of wine is (obviously, given the owner) extensive and reasonably priced, but the welcome is what matters. It's hard to imagine anywhere, even in Italy, where you'll be better looked after, not just by the employees, but by the patrons.

The ideal time to visit? Any evening really, but if you can manage it, the last day of June, before the Oste shuts up shop for the summer, is a good bet. All the regulars – and quite a few irregulars – turn up, some bringing garden furniture to cope with the overflow onto the street. But come whenever you can to enjoy informal Italian urban eating at its best. Pop in for an aperitivo, a quick drink and maybe a snack, stay for a lengthy series of taste sensations, or just pass through quickly for a pudding wine and a chance to chat.

But that still leaves one question. Why does Renzo, a highly successful businessman, choose to spend six evenings a week working in a tucked away wine bar? As he tells it, the idea for the bar came about when a doctor from Todi asked Renzo to recommend a good bottle of wine as a present for his pharmacist. Much discussion later, the doctor left Renzo's wine warehouse with an expensive bottle of Chateau d'Yquem. When the pharmacist dropped by, aiming to return the favour, Renzo asked what he thought of the wine he'd been given. "I don't really like dessert wines," he said. "I gave it to my gardener."

Hence the wine bar. As Renzo sees it, there is an ongoing need to educate people about wine. The Oste della Mal'Ora is a great place to learn.

Opposite: A *degustazione* day at Vini e Capricci, Renzo's wine warehouse, enabling a wide range of both Umbrian wine and food producers to showcase their wares and talk to interested buyers.

Baccalà con ceci Salt Cod with Chickpeas

Renzo explains: "Dried salt cod is probably the only fish used in all regions of Italy,
including those of the mountains". The tastes and flavours of all the ingredients in
this dish complement each other beautifully.

SERVES 1, (GENEROUSLY)
chickpeas: dried (preferably organic)
rosemary
unpeeled garlic
salt cod (100g per person)
extra virgin olive oil
pink peppercorns

Soak the chickpeas in cold water for at least 12 hours, drain and boil in water
with rosemary and a few cloves of unpeeled garlic. Cut the soaked salt cod into
thin slices.

Dress the chickpeas with extra virgin olive oil, rosemary, fresh garlic, freshly
ground salt and pepper. Assemble by laying the salt cod around the edge of the
plate and putting the chickpeas (cold in summer and warm in winter) in the
middle. Garnish with pink peppercorns on the salt cod and further rosemary.

Wine suggestion: White : Arquata Grechetto Colli Martani Adanti. Renzo
explains that "this is produced in Umbria from the grape of the same name.
A pale yellow colour with green reflections. A subtle flavour with an elegant,
persistent, soft fruity perfume with hints of honey and rose."

Piatto Napoli Neapolitan Platter

This isn't so much a recipe as a fantastic array of flavours and textures. Made with fresh Fisciano buffalo mozzarella, Neapolitan salami, and a couscous salad inspired by the cuisine of southern Sicily, it is, Renzo explains, "drawn from the union of local traditions from various parts of southern Italy." The platter can be adapted for summer or winter by the inclusion of anchovies or salami respectively.

SERVES 1, (GENEROUSLY)

150g buffalo mozzarella – fresh, no more than 1 day old
taboulé: salad of couscous flavoured with lemon, extra virgin olive oil, a lot of finely chopped parsley, ripe Pachino tomatoes cut into small pieces, salt

anchovies in oil (recommended for warm weather)
Agerolino salami or salami of your choice (in cold months)

Arrange everything on a plate and serve.

Wine suggestion: White – Fiano di Avellino Mastroberardino. Renzo explains that "this takes its name from the grape of the same name, one of Italy's most ancient grape varieties. Traditionally, the vine was planted amongst hazelnut trees. The wine has a pale yellow colour, with a delicate bouquet and good acidity. The nose detects dried fruit, and the tongue, toasted hazelnuts."

Todi

Todi's Piazza del Popolo, with its cathedral and magnificent medieval buildings, is probably one of the most photographed public spaces in the region. That, however, is not the only reason for its popularity, especially with Anglo-Saxons. The University of Kentucky has repeatedly declared Todi the town with the highest standard of living in the world.

L'Osteria al Duomo
Carmine Iaquinangelo and Alessandra Russo

Osteria al Duomo
via San Lorenzo 1
Todi
T: +39 075 894 4400

Opening hours: 12.30 – 14.30
  and 19.30 – 22.30
Closed: Sun evening and Mon
  lunchtime in summer (15 Jun
  – 1 Sept); Sun evening and
  all day Mon in winter
Holidays: 8 Jan – 8 Feb
Covers: 28

Carmine Iaquinangelo and Alessandra Russo met while working together in Catania in Sicily. Within a few months they decided that they would one day run their own restaurant together.

Osteria al Duomo opened under their management in June 2003. It's small, intimate and civilized, a real refuge from the tourist hubbub that is Todi, despite being only a few steps from the visitor magnet of Piazza del Popolo and, as the name suggests, from the cathedral.

Carmine admits that he and Alessandra came to settle in Todi by pure chance. The intention had been to go to the area around Siena in Tuscany, but when they found their current venue, they liked it immediately. Umbria too appealed to both of them because of its rich supply of top-quality produce. Still, it must be hard for him, a Neapolitan, to live in Umbria where there's no coastline. "It's very difficult," he admits. "Every morning I wake up and think of the sea, but fortunately we're always here so we don't see outside. We just go home to sleep."

Which is hardly surprising when you consider their workload. "We did think of calling it *Ristorante in Due* because there's always just two of us," Carmine says drily. He has worked abroad, including a stint for Raymond Blanc at Le Manoir in Oxford, but says that the work he does here is particularly exhausting. "In the kitchen there is just me. And I'm not proud; I wash the pots and pans after I've cooked".

Which gives you some idea of their dedication. Further evidence comes from their uncompromising approach to quality. A friend of Carmine who was studying agriculture prepared a schedule for him of peak production times for various vegetables and legumes, along with their peak times for taste. However,

Opposite above: Carmine and Alessandra are unapologetic purists, preparing and serving food in what they consider to be the right way.

Opposite below: Small, intimate and civilized, Osteria al Duomo is a real refuge from the tourist hubbub.

along with taste, the aesthetic component of vegetables is critical for Carmine too. "Colours are very important," he says, and he proves it in the selection photographed.

On entering Osteria al Duomo, you walk into a small bar area, but it's a bar area that is more than a drinking space. There is a good choice of wine by the glass, not to mention a fascinating selection of beers, with notes provided on fermentation details and the best food to eat with them. There are also excellent bar snacks. A limited selection maybe – cheeses, hams and grilled vegetables – but quality fare.

That description in some ways fits the restaurant too. The menu is small, offering four to five choices per course, but the food is excellent, and includes meat, fish and vegetarian options. In theory it changes seasonally, but in practice it's at the mercy of Carmine's suppliers. Compromising on quality is out of the question, so if the menu states that a dish features broad beans but they weren't in prime condition that morning, then don't be surprised to see peas – of the best quality, naturally – offered as a substitute.

Nor do they compromise on service. When the pair arrived here there were 44 covers. "It was", says Carmine, "a much more touristy restaurant. We decided to remove a few places because for us it's important to work well with fewer people."

And so they do, few better than Alessandra, who looks after the dining room with flair and friendly professionalism. Carmine acknowledges her contribution to the operation. "Cooks are always seen as being a bit mad, but to wait at tables, to be somebody who is in regular contact with people, you need to have a distinctive character. I could never be in contact with the customers because I'm too touchy." Alessandra emphasises that patience is a necessary virtue, as is being able to cope with different types of people – including the chef. "When you take an order you can't afford to misrepresent the kitchen. It's a constant search for balance," she says. Absolutely, says Carmine. "Only the chef has the right to lose his temper!"

You couldn't imagine Alessandra losing hers. She has worked in Australia, London, Miami and the Channel Islands. Her English is strong and her manner is both welcoming and helpful. The décor is her choice and is a key element of the tranquil atmosphere the couple seek to provide. As much as quality and detail are important to Carmine in the kitchen, the same is true of Alessandra and the dining areas. There are cloth 'rose petals' scattered on each table, along with a single brightly coloured flower at lunchtime which is replaced by a candle for the dinner service. The table linens are cream, the brick ceiling is vaulted and calmness pervades. There's also a fine selection of trad jazz playing gently in the

background, to the great approval of diners.

The pair are unapologetic purists, preparing and serving food in what they consider to be the right way. Carmine likes the challenge of changing each season's dishes every year because he doesn't want to get stuck in the rut of cooking the same things all the time. He concedes, however, that if he's developed a dish that is successful then there is no reason to change it; they are, after all, aware that they are now running a business in the real world. Nevertheless, as far as possible, the aim is, as Carmine puts it, to avoid being a 'typical' restaurant that offers 10 main courses for Eur12, but instead to offer "a small menu but one of quality".

In the meantime, it looks like the pair's dedication to quality over quantity is paying off. As Alessandra puts it: "What's interesting for us is that foreigners who came here last year, have returned this year, some from far away. That gives us great satisfaction." *Ristorante in Due?* Maybe not for long.

Above: Carmine Iaquinangelo working with uncompromising dedication in his kitchen.

Parmigiana di Verdure di Stagione con Mozzarella di Bufala e Basilica

Grilled Vegetables with Buffalo Mozzarella and Basil

One of Carmine's simple but attractive vegetarian dishes.

SERVES 4 – 6

500g courgettes	**salt and pepper as needed**
500g aubergine	**extra virgin olive oil**
500g red peppers (core and seeds removed)	**basil**
	oregano
250g buffalo mozzarella	**grated Parmesan**

Preheat the oven to 240°C, and place a square of greaseproof paper in a baking dish. Cut the vegetables into slices of 5mm thick, brush with olive and grill. In the meantime, slice the mozzarella. Overlap the vegetable slices, mozzarella and basil in a row, alternately on top of the greaseproof paper in the baking tray. Season and sprinkle the grated Parmesan and oregano over each slice, followed by a drizzle of olive oil. Put into the oven for a few minutes, until the vegetables are heated through and the mozzarella starts to melt.

Serve immediately.

Wine suggestion: White – Prosecco or a fruity white, Grechetto Umbro or Sauvignon Blanc

Lasagne alle Ortiche Vegetable Lasagne

Carmine assembles these individually but it can be made on a much bigger scale by putting into a traditional lasagne dish the conventional way with big sheets and then cutting into individual portions. He also varies this by adding a layer of fish along with the tomatoes and aubergines.

SERVES 4

1 kg aubergines	basil
sea salt	parsley
extra virgin olive oil	300g cherry tomatoes
pepper	cane sugar
oregano	sesame seed oil
200g goat's Ricotta	400g lasagne sheets

To prepare the aubergines: preheat the oven to 200°C. Put 1 small aubergine to one side. Cut the rest in half lengthwise and sprinkle over some sea salt, oil, a small amount of pepper and oregano. Cover with foil and put in the oven for 25 minutes. They are ready when a spoon can extract the flesh easily for mashing which should be done with a knife, not a machine. Once mashed, mix in the ricotta with a fork along with some oil, basil and parsley.

To prepare the oven-dried cherry tomatoes: cut them in half vertically and put on a baking tray. Sprinkle over salt, pepper, cane sugar and a drizzle of oil. Put into a 70°C oven for approx an hour.

Cut the remaining aubergine very finely on a mandolin. Dry well on a tea towel, then fry in sesame seed oil on a very low heat. Remove from heat when they have become light brown and crunchy. Keep to one side.

To prepare the lasagne: Reheat the vegetables and put the lasagne sheets on to boil. Assemble individually starting off with a sheet of pasta, then layer on the aubergines and tomatoes alternately, finishing with a pasta sheet. Garnish with the fried aubergine strips.

Wine suggestion: White – Orvieto Classico, Fallanghina

Ristorante Umbria Fausto and Maurizio Todini

Ristorante Umbria
via San Bonaventura 13
Todi
T: +39 075 894 2737

Opening hours: 12.30–14.30
  and 19.30–22.30
Closed: Tues
Holidays: none
Covers: terrace 60;
  dining room 60

"In summer it's a surprise because you come from the historical centre to find this extraordinary view. But that's a characteristic of Todi."

Maurizio Todini is right. Not only the name, but also the terrace at Ristorante Umbria will give you a stunning sense of location. However, the front of the restaurant, situated just off Piazza del Popolo, offers no clue as to the treat that lies in store should you be lucky enough to nab a table outside.

Ristorante Umbria is run by the second generation of the Todini family. The parents of chef Fausto and head waiter Maurizio took over what was a trattoria in 1953. The two brothers have worked together now for nearly 30 years.

The surname is no accident. The brothers and their family have their roots in Todi. Maurizio is particularly emotional about his hometown. "I'm in love with my city," he says. "For me the cathedral is not a tourist monument; it's where my children were baptised."

As for the food, it's traditional and hearty, an approach that seems to have universal appeal; it's not just the tourists who are attracted by the classic Umbrian part of the menu. However, if that's not to your taste don't be put off. The menu changes seasonally and in recent years the vegetarian dishes have increased in popularity. In fact the soups and truffle dishes are always in demand and the brothers have updated the menu over the years to make it less heavy and more appealing to changing preferences for simpler, healthier food.

Does this approach work? Well, people return; many have been doing so for 15 years. In fact, it's a testament to the good time that visitors have here that some tell the brothers that they can recall everything they ate during a visit a decade ago.

Not that Fausto would remember them all. He leaves the business of being

Opposite above: Not only the name, but also the terrace at Ristorante Umbria will give you a stunning sense of location.

Opposite below: "In summer it's a surprise because you come from the historical centre to find this extraordinary view. But that's a characteristic of Todi".

outgoing to Maurizio. There is no sibling rivalry. But then, how could there be? Fausto is diffident and Maurizio can't cook. Or, as Maurizio puts it: "It fascinates me but I only know how to make a few small things. So if someone compliments the food, I make sure that it reaches my brother – at least it stays in the family."

Maurizio is, frankly, selling himself short. Years of experience have made him very good at his job. In the summer, there's a buzzing mix of tourists and locals on the terrace, all enjoying the view, but well sheltered. Maurizio looks after them efficiently and with a minimum of fuss.

Fausto is happier out of the limelight. "It's hard work in the kitchen but it's better to work for yourself," he says. "Some people would see themselves as stuck in a small kitchen, but we have lots of natural light and the view is amazing."

And will a third generation take over? Well, Fausto and Maurizio's children have seen the amount of work involved, or, as Maurizio succinctly puts it, "you need total passion and commitment, because you have very little leisure time".

Sadly, then, it looks as though the hard work that has made this a successful family concern will be the undoing of the family tradition. It might therefore be wise to visit Ristorante Umbria before the brothers retire, although, judging from the way Maurizio spends his free time, that may be some way off. "I love my work," he says. "On Tuesdays when we're closed, I often pop in just to check the tables. It's our home more than our business."

Above left: Head waiter Maurizio looks after diners efficiently and with a minimum of fuss.

Above right: Chef Fausto is happier out of the limelight and admits that it's hard work in the kitchen.

Brasato di Capriolo con Funghi Porcini e Menta
Braised Venison with Porcini Mushrooms and Mint

Venison in red wine is a classic dish but Fausto's inclusion of mint adds a totally new dimension.

SERVES 2

500g venison	**olive oil**
salt and pepper	**cognac**
1 clove garlic	**1 ¹/₂ litres full-bodied red wine**
30g mint	**200g porcini (caps), cut into strips**

Place the venison in a large pan, season with salt and pepper, garlic, half the mint and oil. Cook on a moderate heat for 45 minutes, then bathe in cognac and wait 5 minutes. Cover everything with the red wine, and boil until the liquid has reduced by ¹/₃.

Sauté the mushroom caps in a pan with oil and salt. Cut the venison into 6 slices and place on a serving platter. Put the mushroom caps on top of the meat and pour over some of the reduced wine. Garnish with the remaining mint.

Wine suggestion: Red – Sagrantino di Montefalco

Budino Freddo di Castagne Cold Chestnut Pudding

An ingenious way of using up surplus chestnuts – and a striking one, thanks to the candied fruit decoration.

SERVES 6–8

500ml milk
1 vanilla pod
pinch of salt
400g shelled chestnuts
50g sugar
80g toasted almonds, cooled and
    ground

gelatine as necessary
150ml whipped cream
80g candied fruit, chopped and
    marinated in some kirsch
additional whipped cream and fruit
    for decoration (optional)

Grease a mould or baking tin and line with clingfilm, generously overlapping the rim to facilitate removal of the pudding.

Bring the milk, with the vanilla and a pinch of salt, to the boil. Add the chestnuts and cook over a moderate heat to the point where they can be finely minced (remove the vanilla pod before passing through the mincer). Return the fine puree (leaving any bits behind) to the pan, add the sugar and reduce slightly. Away from the heat, soak the gelatine sheets in water as directed, and mix into the hot chestnut purée along with the ground almonds and whipped cream. Pour half the mixture into the mould, sprinkle over the candied fruit, then pour in the remaining mixture. Put in the fridge for several hours until set firmly.

To serve, turn upside down onto a plate, remove the mould, peel away the clingfilm, and decorate with the whipped cream and fruit if so desired.

Wine suggestion: Dessert – Vin Santo, Umbria or Moscato di Pantelleria

Regional Specialities

Umbrians adore their local specialities. They are not alone. Their high-quality foodstuffs, an essential part of the culinary heritage of Umbria, are cherished by both the locals and an ever-increasing worldwide audience. Castellucio lentils, truffles, fagiolina di Trasimeno, farro, Trevi celery, Colfiorito potatoes, the rich, green olive oil, wine and all manner of pork products are sought after by both inhabitants and visitors.

Here is a brief look at some of these specialities. The businesses high-lighted here are not large-scale undertakings. They are predominantly family-run operations where, despite often successful export operations, personal involvement, not commercial streamlining, is the order of the day.

Ansuini Prosciutto

F.lli Ansuini
via Anicia 105
Norcia
T: +39 0743 816 643

The Fratelli Ansuini shop in Norcia is a pork-lover's dream: an amazing selection of hams, sausages and salamis is accompanied by tubs of beans and lentils, an extensive display of truffles and a tempting array of cheeses.

Vittorio Ansuini knows the exact provenance of all his hams, which are processed in the family plant a short way beyond the walls of Norcia. "Traceability is important," he explains, "especially if your reputation is based on quality. Any serious consumer of food understands that you get what you pay for." And any serious consumer would believe him: his whole family is involved in the business in some way, and has been for three generations.

It takes 16–18 months to produce the raw cured ham known as prosciutto. The fresh prosciutto joints are first salted by hand and then put in cold storage for 21 days where they are freshly resalted every seven days, always by hand. They are then left for 15 days without salt, and then for a further 80–90 days in an environment with minimum humidity. Following these phases they are washed in a 'bath' and then taken immediately to a drying room, where not only temperature – 21°C – but also humidity – 60 per cent – are much higher. At this point, pepper is added around the bone. The final phase is one of rest for nine to ten months, although during the final four months pork fat is added.

The processing plant is high-tech where it needs to be but still has the feel of a family-run business where everyone joins in and feels committed to the quality of the final product. Walter Ansuini, Vittorio's son, enthuses not only about the hams but about the production process that makes them prosciutto. His favourite pork product isn't hard to guess. "I love sausages but I prefer prosciutto. I eat it at least once a day. Hey, I'm from Norcia, what do you expect?"

Opposite above: Vittorio Ansuini surrounded by an amazing selection of hams, sausages, beans, lentils, truffles and cheeses in his shop in Norcia.

Opposite below: The final phase of prosciutto production at the Ansuini family plant.

Antonelli Vineyard

Localita San Marco
Montefalco
T: +39 0742 379158
W: www.antonelli
     sanmarco.it

Public wine tasting and sales:
Mon–Fri (except public holidays) 08.30 – 12.30 and 14.30 – 18.30 and Sat mornings
Wine tasting is free but groups no bigger than 20 can be accommodated

The Antonelli vineyard and azienda is about three kilometres outside Montefalco. Approximately 200,000 bottles of wine a year are produced by Antonelli, with its Montefalco Rosso being almost obligatory drinking in the area. Sagrantino Passito and Sagrantino Secco are the jewels in the crown here but Brunella Schienalunga, who works in the azienda, explains that "Montefalco locals mean the Passito when they refer to Sagrantino as they tend not to drink the dry (secco) Sagrantino. In fact some are unaware of the existence of the dry version."

Cicchetti Farro

Azienda Agricola Cicchetti snc
Ruscio Monteleone di Spoleto
T: +39 0743 755 841

Farro is an ancient grain, referred to in the Bible and credited with having kept the Roman army marching. It is also healthy and wholesome, properties that are seeing it find favour among the modern inhabitants of Italy.

The Cicchetti family have been growing and processing the *Triticum Durum Dicoccum* variety of farro since the 1960s in Monteleone di Spoleto in the Valnerina. Only 1,000kg of farro per hectare is produced here, less than the usual yield as the crop is organic. There is one harvest per year; it begins in August and takes 25 days.

Most members of the family work for the business in some way. Daniel, who is 21, used to help out after school and has now been working full time for over a year.

Daniels's favourite way of eating farro is in a soup with chickpeas, beans and lentils, all products cultivated, wrapped and sold by the family. However, for those with a sweeter tooth, the family has started making plain and chocolate-covered galettes, or farro versions of the rice cake.

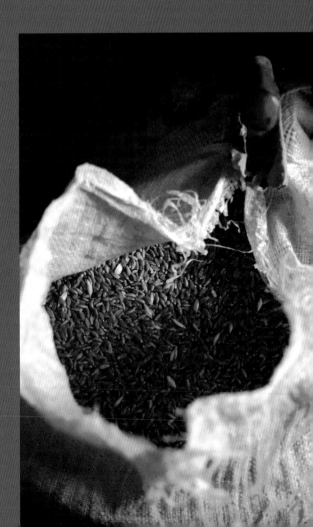

Agricola Torre Olivola

Giorgio Shaw
Torre Gentile
Todi
T: +39 348 9295 176

About 14km outside Todi, deep in the countryside is the Agricola La Torre Olivola. This is, by porcine standards, a five-star residence, but then the Cinta Senese is no ordinary pig. An ancient breed, originating from Tuscany, it was close to extinction in the 1950s but there has been a concerted effort to ensure its survival. Its white *cinta* (belt) is its most obvious characteristic. Giorgio Shaw, who manages the operation, explains that there are now 500 Cinta Senese pigs in Umbria. Many families in the region have five or six. He, however, has 300.

The registration process is strict. Newborns must be logged at younger than 20 days, but if their mother is not registered as a Cinta Senese, nor can the piglets be. A round disc is affixed to the ear to denote registration: a pig with a fully circular 'earring' is a perfect specimen; if it's not quite perfect then a piece will be cut off the 'earring' so that it's not circular. If there is no 'earring' then it's not a pure Cinta Senese ("or one of the other pigs has chewed it off !" explains Giorgio).

Marco Lipparoni has always loved animals and has bred all sorts but pigs are his favourites, and he's an authority. He understands them and is particularly attentive to coughs – Cinta Senese are prone to weak lungs. Both he and Giorgio are particularly proud of the two studs, Giorgione and Napoleone. who have been responsible for increasing the herd from four pigs. "Giorgione was very quiet to start with, but then he went crazy with all the women," says Giorgio. Which may explain why he's not so crazy now: all 300kg of him looks utterly exhausted.

These pigs take 14 months to reach a weight of 120kg (the pig farm convention is eight months). This means that the meat they produce is not cheap but it has the most extraordinary flavour. The salamis and sausages *sott'olio* (in oil) that Giorgio sells are especially – in fact outstandingly – tasty.

Opposite above: A round disc affixed to the ear denotes registration of pure Cinta Senese; it is possible for two pure-breed parents to have impure piglets. They live like wild boar and forage for food and roots in the ground.

Opposite below: Giorgio Shaw, manager of the Agricola Torre Olivola.

Frantoio Mancianti

via della Parrocchia 20
San Feliciano
T: +39 075 847 6045

A fundamental building block of the local diet, Umbrian olive oil is noted for its green colour. Umbrians value their olive oil highly and tend to be well versed on the differences between oils from the various microclimates in their region.

Many non-farming families have a small number of olive trees, and continue the tradition of taking their olives to a local mill and receiving a percentage of the oil produced in return for processing. One such *frantoio* (oil press) that continues this tradition is Frantoio Mancianti on Lake Trasimeno. Suppliers need to bring a minimum of 400kg olives to be processed; 20 per cent of the oil produced will be returned to them.

Mancianti produces three different qualities of oil, the best known of which is *l'affiorato* (a term devised by Alfredo Mancianti and now widely used), which denotes cold pressed oil left in terracotta pots to filter naturally so that the sediment settles at the bottom. The oil is skimmed by hand and then bottled. The period from November to spring sees the most intense activity at the frantoio.

Assisi

La Fortezza

Behind the fountain in Piazza del Comune, on the Taverna dei Consoli side (opposite the Pinacoteca Comunale) is a road of steps – Vicolo della Fortezza. Up these, just before the bend on RHS is La Fortezza.

La Stalla

From the gate Porta Cappuccini, La Stalla is a short (15 minute) walk along the main road in the direction of Eremo delle Carceri. Take the gravel path alongside the main road, turning right at the 'Camping Fontemaggio' sign. Or, from the Porta Cappuccini, take the pedestrian only road between the main road and Viale Giovanni XXIII.

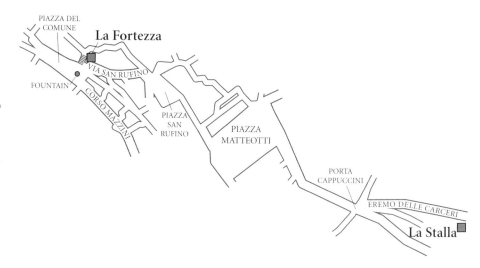

Bevagna

Ottavius

From Piazza Silvestri (with Corso Giaciomo Matteotti behind you) turn left along Via G. Pagliochini to reach Largo Gramsci. Ottavius is on the LHS just past Caffe del Teatro. Alternatively, from Piazza Silvestri walk past the tourist office along Via Gonfalone, and Ottavius is on your RHS.

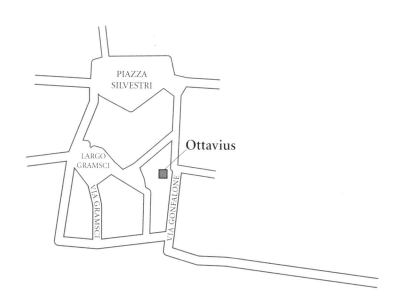

Castiglione del Lago

Vinolento

From Piazza Giuseppe Mazzini walk along
Via Vittoria Emanuele. Carry on past Piazza
Cesare Caporali (on RHS) and Vinolento is
on the RHS just before Piazza Gramsci.

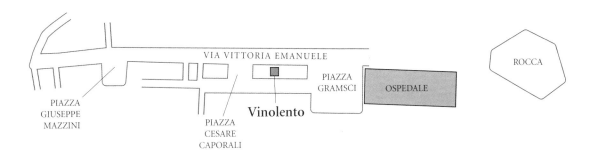

Citta di Castello

Il Postale

Just outside the city walls, take the Strada
Apecchiese (signposted "Apecchio and Fano –
Acqualagna SS257"). About 100m on the LHS
is a grey metal gate marked 'Il Postale'.

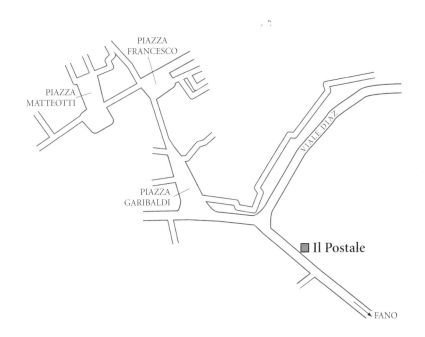

Ferentillo

Il Cantico

From Terni take the Terni Est exit and follow signs to Visso, Norcia on the SS209 Valnerina for 20km. 3km after the village of Ferentillo, turn left following the sign 'Residenza d'Epoca Abbazia S.Pietro in Valle'. Follow signs to the Abbey car park; the restaurant is on the LHS of the gate to the Abbey.

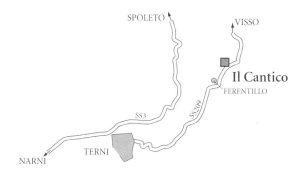

Foligno

Il Bacco Felice

From Piazza della Repubblica (with your back to Bottega Barbanera) go left to Via Giuseppe Garibaldi through Piazza Matteotti. Carry on past Corso Cavour on RHS. Road becomes narrow and one-way with no pavement, but cars allow for pedestrians on both sides of the street. On LHS there's a Caffe and Pasticeria "Dal 1795 Muzzi Antica Pasticceria" and just past this on LHS, is Salvo's door. The entrance is not very obvious; the name "Il Bacco Felice" is on a small board at the bottom of the window and there's usually a yucca plant outside. If you reach Piazza Garibaldi with the statue of Garibaldi, you've gone too far and need to go back about 7–8 doors.

Villa Roncallli

Going into Foligno from Sant Eraclio: along the Viale Roma, just after the 'Foligno' sign, on RHS (shortly after the Esso station) there is a white warehouse type building with blue and yellow insignia, 'Dico Discount Alimentare'. The foliage-covered entrance to Villa Roncalli is on the RHS immediately after this.

If leaving Foligno follow signs to S Eraclio (to the SE). At the large roundabout take sign to S Eraclio. Continue past the road on LHS leading to shops and signposted to cemetery and just after this is the foliage-covered entrance to Villa Roncalli on LHS.

If you pass a white warehouse building "Dico Discount Alimentare" or an Esso petrol station, you've gone too far.

Note that the entrance to Villa Roncalli is not obvious. Although there are signs either side of the entrance (a tree lined road) they are partly covered by shrubbery.

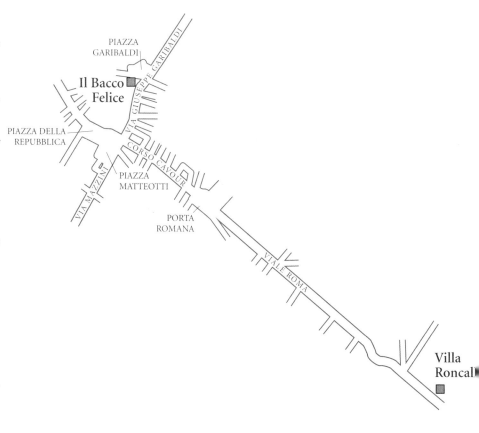

Gubbio

La Fornace di Mastro Giorgio

Go along Corso Garibaldi until reach Piazza Oderisi. Opposite the tourist office, the road with steps going up is via Felice Cavallotti. Go up. Cross over to Via Savelli della Porta with Palazzo della Porta on your RHS and go up the sweeping steps of Via Mastro Giorgio. La Fornace di Mastro Giorgio and La Madia di Giuseppe are on RHS towards top just before Via XX Settembre.

Montefalco

L'Alchimista

L'Alchimista is to be found in the Piazza del Comune just next to Via Porta Camiano; 2 doors along from the Tourist Office, on the same side as the Teatro San Filippo Neri.

Norcia

Il Granaro del Monte

From Porta Romana go along Corso Sertorio to Piazza Vittorio Veneto (the theatre is here). The next turning on RHS, (which is the 5th on the RHS from Porta Romana) right in front of Piazza San Benedetto, is a small road that goes back on itself, Via Alfieri. Granaro del Monte is down here on the LHS.

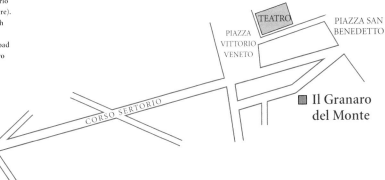

Orvieto

L'Antica Trattoria dell'Orso

Walking along Corso Cavour shortly before Piazza della Repubblica, there is a small turning on the RHS (opposite Via Garibaldi); this is Via della Misericordia. Down here on RHS, just before Piazza Ascanio Vitozzi, is L'Antica Trattoria dell'Orso.

L'Asino d'Oro

From the cathedral go down Via del Duomo to the junction with Corso Cavour; turn left and then immediately right down a small alleyway – Vicolo del Popolo (this is small but is the first RH turn diagonally opposite Via de Cartari (this is pedestrianised as is not big enough for even 1 small car to go down). The alleyway opens up into a very small square and on the LHS is Asino d'Oro. Note that there are some interesting shops down this pedestrianised road.

Alternatively, from the Piazza del Popolo, the side of the square opposite the Palazzo del Popolo. On the block next to the Grande Albergo Reale, there's a small grey archway with a pedestrianised sign (Area Pedonale) – between Gabetti Estate Agency and Abbigliamento Alberto (an old fashioned clothing shop with a table of boxes of shirts, rolls of fabric and a rail of dresses outside). There's a small sign up high inside this arch, marking it as Vicolo del Popolo. Carry along here until opens up onto a small square area and L'Asino d'Oro is on RHS.

Le Grotte del Funaro

From Piazza della Repubblica, take Via della Loggia de' Mercanti (between Via Filippeschi and shops next to the Police Station – Generali building next to road). Carry on to end of road with Palazzo Piccolomini hotel on the RHS of Piazza de Ranieri. Turn right and take the higher road, Via Ripa Serancia and carry along here for a short way. The restaurant is under the arch on your LHS just before you get to the wall of the town with amazing views.

Perugia

L'Osteria del Gambero

In Piazza IV Novembre with your back to the tourist office, facing the Cattedrale di San Lorenzo, go left down Via (Maesta) delle Volte. Carry on round to the right downhill under the arch until you reach the small Piazza Cavallotti. Continue round to the right (hug the wall) and the first road on RHS is Via Baldeschi. Del Gambero is a short way along here on LHS.

La Piazzetta

From Corso Vannucci, facing the fountain, just before the Galleria Nazionale dell'Umbria go left down Via dei Priori. Carry on downhill past shops on either side. Get to crossroads with Via della Cupa and turn left; take the first right into Via Deliziosa and the restaurant is on the right.

Pigge/Trevi

La Taverna del Pescatore

By road: from Foligno take the motorway south towards Spoleto and Terni. Take the Trevi exit and at the T-junction traffic lights turn right towards Pigge. Continue for approx 3.5km and look for road signs for the Taverna del Pescatore, passing the Agip petrol station and the Tartufi Funghi restaurant on the right. Take the slip road, which runs parallel to the main road, to the right for approx 400m, following signs to the restaurant. Finally take a sharp right hand turn into the car park of the Taverna.

Scheggino

Del Ponte (no map)

From the car park in Piazza del Mercato, walk over the Fiume Nera using the Franco Malfatti bridge. Turn right and walk along via di Borgo parallel with the canal. The hotel and restaurant Del Ponte are just in front of you on the RHS.

Spello

La Bastiglia

Enter Spello through Porta Montanara and shortly after there is a car park on the LHS. La Bastiglia is just after here on the LHS.

If you're walking from the centre of town, just keep on walking up from Piazza della Repubblica, along Via Garibaldi, along Via Giulia to Piazza Valle Gloria. La Bastiglia is on the RHS.

La Cantina

Go up Via Cavour, to Piazza Giacomo Matteotti with the tourist office on RHS. Road narrows before reaching Piazza della Repubblica and just after it narrows, La Cantina is on the RHS.

Spoleto

Il Panciolle

Come down the steps in front of the Duomo and at the bottom of the steps go back on yourself to the left and down Via del Duomo (the name is not marked until the end), go left at the bottom and continue for a short while. Just before Largo Muzio Clementi there are downward steps on the RHS which lead to Il Panciolle on LHS.

Osteria del Matto

In the Piazza del Mercato, facing the fountain, opposite the Self Service del Mercato Bar, there is a small arch on LHS, 'Vicolo del Mercato' with a no entry sign (between a fruit and veg shop and a souvenir/newsagents "Souvenir Articoli Regalo, Tabachi, Giornali"). Go through here and directly in front of you is Osteria del Matto.

Terni

Oste della Mal'Ora

From Piazza Europa walk NNE to Piazza della Repubblica and carry on along Corso Cornelio Tacito (predominantly pedestrian thoroughfare) on the LHS, on corner of via Giuseppe Petroni is the Caffe Pazzaglia. Turn right down Via del Tribunale. At the T-junction with Corso Vecchio turn left. The Corso widens to a small, unnamed square with Drogheria VinoVino on the RHS. Go back on yourself to the right into the Via 3 Archi. L'Oste is on the RHS.

Todi

Osteria al Duomo

Facing the Duomo, just level with its steps, on the RHS is Via S. Lorenzo and a sign to Osteria al Duomo, Ristorante, Enoteca. The restaurant is a few steps down here on the LHS.

Ristorante Umbria

At the south end of the Piazza del Popolo (the tourist info and Palazzo del Popolo end, opposite end from the Duomo), face the Duomo and turn right under the arch immediately after the Tourist Office (unnamed) in the direction of the Bagni (Baths). By the time you reach the baths, you'll see the restaurant in front of you.

Index

Acknowledgements

The author would like to thank: Everybody who has contributed excitedly and generously to this project, in particular:

My husband Dan, with whom I have shared so many wonderful meals in Umbria over the years. Without his encouragement this book would never have been started, and without his boundless enthusiasm, constant inspiration and support it might never have been finished; all the individuals, chefs, owners and serving staff, featured in this book for their time, willingness to help in every way possible and warm welcomes; the Bonny Day Publishing editorial board: Elizabeth Canning and Scott Steedman for their inventiveness and ability to challenge all assumptions; Vaughan O'Grady for being an encouraging and constructive editor; the recipe testers: Andrea Bothamley, Pete Livesey, Joanne Morton, Susan Searle and Jill Sheppard, for going way beyond the call of duty and struggling with a huge number of culinary challenges; Jane Bonser for tenaciously and ingeniously sourcing ingredients; Caroline Shaw for not only proofing and indexing with such flair but for maintaining her status as the greatest drinking partner after all these years; Peter Dawson and Tom Green at Grade Design for contributing so much more than artistic and graphic creativity; Tom Coulson and Martin Darlison at Encompass Graphics for producing stylish maps in record time; Bruno Roncarati for Italian assistance in London; Cathy Colecchi for lateral thinking from New York; Fiona Rough for all sorts of advice from Abu Dhabi; Michael Taylor and Tim Flach for solving numerous problems; Richard Bone, Jamie McFarlane, Adam Morley and Mark Sharp at Sho Design for innovative creativity and the most eclectic choice of studio background music heard in Camden Town; Renzo and Paola Franceschini, Andrea Barbaccia and Beppe Neri of the Oste della Mal'Ora in Terni for giving so much help, providing great introductions and turning every visit into a party, and, Eddie Jacob who worked so much harder than could reasonably be expected, for stunning shots, making it all look effortless despite onerous working conditions and keeping it fun. His ability to finish every plate of food he photographed, can only be marvelled at – shoots, eats and leaves...

The photographer would like to thank:

All the restaurant owners and chefs for graciously giving full access to all parts of their kitchens and restaurants. It was an honour and privilege to be invited into their lives, and I hope they feel the end results have done them and their work justice.